Cambridge

Elements in Public Economics
edited by
Robin Boadway
Queen's University
Frank A. Cowell
The London School of Economics and Political Science
Massimo Florio
University of Milan

TAX POLICY

Principles and Lessons

Robin Boadway

Queen's University

Katherine Cuff

McMaster University

CAMBRIDGE
UNIVERSITY PRESS

CAMBRIDGE
UNIVERSITY PRESS

University Printing House, Cambridge CB2 8BS, United Kingdom

One Liberty Plaza, 20th Floor, New York, NY 10006, USA

477 Williamstown Road, Port Melbourne, VIC 3207, Australia

314–321, 3rd Floor, Plot 3, Splendor Forum, Jasola District Centre,
New Delhi – 110025, India

103 Penang Road, #05-06/07, Visioncrest Commercial, Singapore 238467

Cambridge University Press is part of the University of Cambridge.

It furthers the University's mission by disseminating knowledge in the pursuit of
education, learning, and research at the highest international levels of excellence.

www.cambridge.org
Information on this title: www.cambridge.org/9781108949453
DOI: 10.1017/9781108954426

First published 2022

A catalogue record for this publication is available from the British Library.

ISBN 978-1-108-94945-3 Paperback
ISSN 2516-2276 (online)
ISSN 2516-2268 (print)

Tax Policy

Principles and Lessons

Elements in Public Economics

DOI: 10.1017/9781108954426
First published online: April 2022

Robin Boadway
Queen's University

Katherine Cuff
McMaster University

Author for correspondence: Robin Boadway, boadwayr@econ.queensu.ca

Abstract: Tax policies are informed by principles developed in the tax theory and policy literature. This Element surveys the policy lessons that emerge from optimal tax analysis since the 1970s. We begin with the evolution of tax policy principles from the comprehensive income approach to the expenditure tax approach to normative tax analysis based on social welfare maximization. We recount key results from the optimal income tax analysis inspired by Mirrlees and extended by Diamond to the extensive-margin approach. We emphasize analytical techniques that yield empirically relevant concepts and show the equity–efficiency trade-off at the heart of tax policy. We discuss various conceptual issues with social welfare maximization, including interdependent utilities, heterogeneous preferences, behavioural economics, social norms and the source of the social welfare function and their implications for optimal taxation. We also extend the analysis to recent literature incorporating involuntary unemployment and policies like welfare and unemployment insurance.

Keywords: tax policy, optimal taxation, social welfare maximization, redistribution, income taxation

JEL classifications: H21, H23, H24, I38, J68

ISBNs: 9781108949453 (PB), 9781108954426 (OC)
ISSNs: 2516-2276 (online), 2516-2268 (print)

Contents

1 Introduction

The choice of a tax system is among the most important economic decisions governments make. Tax revenues make up on average roughly one-third of gross domestic product (GDP) across the Organisation for Economic Co-operation and Development (OECD) countries. Taxes influence key economic and social outcomes, including productivity, employment and growth; income and wealth distribution; international and intranational mobility of labour and capital; innovation; and social mobility and stability. Although their details differ, tax systems exhibit similar features across countries and continue to evolve in common ways. These broad similarities can be partly attributed to common circumstances facing different countries. Globalization and competitiveness pressures weigh on all of them. The evolution of inequality of income and wealth has proceeded in comparable ways. The industrial structures of OECD economies have increasingly tilted away from manufacturing toward services, and sectors relying on information technology and intellectual property have blossomed. Labour forces have become more educated and diverse, and large multinational corporations that are relatively footloose now dominate the industrial landscape.

Tax policy is the result of political decision-making, but it is informed and judged by tax policy principles. The applications of these principles unavoidably involve value judgments and social norms that vary from country to country, thus affecting the way they are applied, but the established set of tax principles are widely accepted. These principles are based on the voluminous body of tax analysis built up over the years and continually evolving. Policymakers are exposed to the results of tax analysis partly through their advisors in government and in political parties. The implications of the current state of tax analysis for tax policy circulate widely through the tax reform commissions that have been established in various countries from time to time. Examples of these include the UK Royal Commission on the Taxation of Profits and Income (1955), the Royal Commission on Taxation (1966) in Canada, the United States Treasury (1977), the Meade Report (1978), the President's Advisory Panel on Federal Tax Reform (2005), the Australian Treasury (2010) and Mirrlees et al. (2011) in the United Kingdom.

Actual tax reforms adopted in OECD countries reflect these evolving principles to varying extents, and practices implemented in some countries often serve as examples that spread to others. One only has to think of the worldwide adaptation of the value-added tax (VAT) as an example. France adopted a broad-based VAT in 1958, followed by West Germany in 1968 and all other European

Union countries shortly thereafter. By 2018, 166 countries had adopted a VAT, including all OECD countries except the USA.

The intent of this Element is to recount the tax policy implications that emerge from the tax theory literature. We begin with a summary of how tax design principles have evolved over time before discussing the key results from the optimal income tax analysis inspired by Mirrlees (1971) and extended by Diamond (1980) to the extensive-margin approach. We emphasize the analytical techniques that yield empirically relevant concepts and show the equity–efficiency trade-off at the heart of tax policy. We also summarize the evidence about the behavioural responses to redistributive taxation and the evidence in support of the social welfare functions adopted. We outline the implications for tax policy of more realistic labour market considerations. This includes making wages endogenous and allowing for involuntary unemployment. We consider the consequences of recent findings in behavioural economics for tax-transfer policy. Finally, we summarize the tax policy implications of optimal tax analysis.

This Element complements three others. Gordon and Sarada (2019) focuses on corporation income taxation, while Christiansen and Smith (2021) provide a treatment of commodity taxation. The closest one to ours is Tanninen et al. (2019), who study optimal income taxation. Our Element also treats optimal income taxation but with a different orientation. In addition to outlining the underpinnings of the social welfare–maximizing approach to optimal income taxation, we consider extensions such as the extensive-margin approach to labour supply, involuntary unemployment and behavioural approaches, and we emphasize the policy implications of optimal tax analysis.

2 Evolving Principles of Tax Policy

In the public finance literature, there have been three dominant approaches to choosing the tax structure. The *ability-to-pay approach*, reflected in Musgrave's (1959) treatise, dominated the literature until the 1960s. The *personal expenditure tax approach* introduced by Kaldor (1955) was advocated by the US Treasury Blueprints (1977) and the Meade Report (1978). The optimal tax revolution formalized by Mirrlees (1971) and Diamond and Mirrlees (1971) changed the focus of normative tax theory to a social welfare–optimizing approach, or what we shall loosely refer to as the *utilitarian approach*. It is utilitarian in the sense that social welfare is based on individual utilities aggregated into a social welfare function. Recently, a fourth approach based on the notion of *equality-of-opportunity* has been introduced by Roemer (1998) and

Fleurbaey and Maniquet (2011), though its implications for actual tax policy are still in the process of being developed.

In recent years, the tax policy and tax design principles have been dominated by the utilitarian approach, and much of our analysis will be based on it. To put the utilitarian approach into context, it is useful to begin with a brief outline of the different approaches.

2.1 Ability-to-Pay Approach

The ability-to-pay doctrine is based on the idea that the taxes individuals pay should be governed by the economic resources they have at their disposal. Two key features of ability-to-pay distinguish it from other approaches. First, ability-to-pay depends on one's command over resources and not how one chooses to use them. This resource-based emphasis distinguishes it from the utilitarian approach, where tax liabilities are based on utility as determined by individual behaviour. Second, tax liabilities are not related to the uses to which the taxes are put, especially to the benefits one receives from public goods and services. This distinguishes the ability-to-pay principle from benefit taxation associated with Wicksell (1896), according to which taxes are assigned based on benefits received. The benefit principle is challenging to implement and eschews any redistributive role for taxation.

Two operational issues confront the ability-to-pay principle: how should ability-to-pay be measured, and how should taxes vary with ability-to-pay? The standard measure of ability-to-pay is *comprehensive income* developed by Schanz (1896), Haig (1921) and Simons (1938). Comprehensive income parallels Hicks' (1946) notion of income, which is defined as the maximum individuals could consume annually without changing their wealth, or $Y = C + \Delta A$, where Y is income, C is consumption and ΔA is the change in assets or saving. This definition is based on the sum of the uses of income, and through the individual's budget constraint, it is equivalent to the sum of the sources of income, since $Y = E + rA + I$, where E is earnings, rA is capital income assuming a rate of return of r and I is net inheritances.

Some conceptual issues in the definition of Y are worth highlighting. First, consumption and income include items that involve market transactions: they do not include household production, leisure or items obtained by barter. Consumption also includes consumption services obtained from consumer durables that have been purchased. Thus, consumer durables are not included in asset wealth W, and the return on consumer durables is treated as consumption rather than asset income. Similarly, human capital is not included in asset wealth, and the returns to human capital are included in earnings. The rate of return r includes not just normal market returns but also returns to risk-taking and windfall gains. Another conceptual issue concerns bequests, inheritances and other voluntary transfers. While the receipt of such transfers constitutes a change in wealth, giving them may or may not be considered as an act of consumption. Whichever it is, it has implications for tax liabilities under comprehensive income taxation as well as under the other approaches discussed in Sections 2.2 and 2.3.

The second issue is how tax liabilities should vary with ability-to-pay. Some principles have been dominant. One is *horizontal equity*, or the equal treatment of equals. Horizontal equity holds that individuals who are equally well off before taxes and transfers should be equally well off in their presence (Musgrave, 1959). Though this seems innocuous, it becomes murkier when the use of tax revenues is taken into account. Horizontal equity of government decisions entails that equally well-off individuals should remain equally well off after both taxation and government expenditures, which is a demanding standard. Extending the principle of horizontal equity to a federal context is even more demanding. Requiring equal treatment of equals who reside in different regions of a federation is difficult, given that sub-national levels of government choose different policies. In the fiscal federalism literature, horizontal equity is typically invoked in potential terms to inform the design of intergovernmental equalization transfers. The argument is that transfers should be designed so that different sub-national governments have the capacity to provide comparable public services at comparable tax rates, even if they choose not to do so (Boadway and Shah, 2009).

Another general idea is *vertical equity*, which suggests that individuals who have greater ability-to-pay should face appropriately higher tax burdens. The question is how to establish what burdens are appropriate. The principle commonly turned to is *equal sacrifice*, which suggests that the loss of income due to taxes should be comparable for individuals with different initial incomes. Musgrave (1959) distinguished three notions of equal sacrifice. First, *equal absolute sacrifice* of incomes would lead to a regressive tax system in the sense that average tax rates would fall with income.

A second notion is *equal proportionate sacrifice*, which, when applied to incomes, amounts to proportional income taxation. The Royal Commission on Taxation (1966) added to this the idea that there is a level of non-discretionary expenditures that all persons require for the necessities of living. Incomes necessary to finance non-discretionary expenditures should be exempt from taxation, and equal sacrifice should apply only to incomes above that. Assuming equal proportional income sacrifice on non-discretionary income leads to a *linear progressive income tax*, where tax liabilities T are given by $T = t(Y - N)$, where Y is income, t is the tax rate, and N is nondiscretionary income.

A third notion is *equal marginal sacrifice,* whereby taxes are allocated among individuals such that their marginal loss from the last increment of taxation is the same. If equal marginal sacrifice is defined in terms of utility, and if utility is strictly concave in income, taxation would be progressive even in the absence of an exemption for non-discretionary income. This interpretation of equal marginal sacrifice takes us into the realm of utilitarianism, which we discuss in Section 2.3.

Before turning to that, there is a distinction between equal marginal sacrifice and the other two notions of equal sacrifice that has been emphasized by Weinzierl (2014). Under both equal absolute and equal proportional sacrifices, taxation depends on the initial position of taxpayers. Higher pre-tax incomes mitigate liability for higher taxation, especially in the case of equal absolute sacrifice. In effect, the tax system gives property rights to individuals for their pre-tax incomes and bases taxation on costs of deviating from the initial position (a stance defended by Feldstein, 1976, 2012). This is unlike equal marginal sacrifice where marginal utility of income at the pre-tax allocation does not count.

2.2 Personal Expenditures Approach

The ability-to-pay approach emphasizes an individual's command over resources or comprehensive income. Kaldor (1955) interpreted comprehensive income as a measure of one's contribution to the economy. He argued that instead individuals should be taxed according to what they took out for personal use, which he argued was their consumption expenditures. He proposed using aggregate consumption expenditures over the tax year as the base for direct personal taxation. This idea was taken up by the US Treasury (1977) and the Meade Report (1978), and more recently by the Mirrlees Review (Mirrlees et al., 2011). It has become an important benchmark alternative to income taxation.

Taxing personal consumption expenditures directly would be very challenging since it would require individuals to report their total consumption annually. Fortunately, there are feasible tax bases that are equivalent to consumption. One follows immediately from the individual's annual budget constraint: $C = Y - S$, where $S = \Delta A$ is saving, which can be positive or negative. This is called the *tax-deferred approach* to expenditure taxation. Each year individuals deduct savings from the incomes they report. Sheltered savings are held in an account and accumulate tax-free. When the account is drawn down, funds removed are reported as income. In many countries, private pension funds are taxed on a tax-deferred basis.

A second approach is the *tax-prepaid approach*, whose equivalence to consumption is a consequence of the individual's intertemporal budget constraint. Over the life cycle, the present value of earnings plus windfall gains (including net inheritances) equals the present value of consumption. Thus, if the individual reported earnings plus windfall gains, an expenditure tax base would apply in present value terms. In this case, the tax base under the tax-prepaid approach would be equivalent to that under the tax-deferred approach. However, tax liabilities would occur later in the life cycle with tax deferment, and the present value of tax liabilities would differ if tax rates differed over time. In practice, tax systems that use the tax-prepaid approach include only earnings and not windfall gains or returns to risk.

An indirect consumption tax system, such as a general VAT, is equivalent to a proportional tax on consumption. Its base is analogous to the tax-deferred base. Expenditure tax systems could be a mixture of tax-deferred direct taxation, tax-prepaid direct taxation and indirect consumption taxation. Moreover, taxpayers could have the discretion to choose the proportions of their assets to hold in tax-deferred and tax-prepaid form. As such, they could smooth their tax liabilities over the life cycle and thereby reduce their tax liabilities in the face of a progressive tax rate structure. Although pure consumption expenditure tax systems are exceedingly rare, many countries have hybrid systems combining an income tax system with a VAT and with the ability to shelter some savings in either tax-deferred or tax-prepaid assets.

Like the ability-to-pay approach, the expenditure tax approach advocated by Kaldor (1955) was not grounded in individual preferences or utility. Subsequent advocates of expenditure taxation, such as the US Treasury (1977), did evoke an efficiency-based welfare cost argument in its support. The argument was that by taxing returns to saving, future consumption is taxed at a higher rate than present consumption. This so-called double taxation of future consumption and the deadweight loss it entails can be avoided by consumption expenditure taxation. However, this alleged superiority of consumption over income taxation on efficiency grounds does not withstand scrutiny when one takes into account leisure as a commodity of choice along with goods. The utilitarian approach does that.

2.3 Utilitarian Approach

Rather than basing tax liabilities on ability-to-pay or total consumption, the utilitarian approach bases taxes on an index of an individual's well-being or utility. More precisely, the ideal tax system maximizes a social welfare function of the form:

$$SWF \equiv W\left(n^1 u^1\left(\mathbf{x}^1\right), \ldots, n^h u^h\left(\mathbf{x}^h\right), \ldots, n^H u^H\left(\mathbf{x}^H\right)\right), \tag{1}$$

where $\mathbf{x}^h = \left(x_0^h, \ldots, x_i^h, \ldots, x_m^h\right)$ is a vector of commodities consumed by each individual of type h, $h = 1, \ldots, H$, and n^h is the number of type $-h$ individuals. The $m + 1$ commodities include both goods and leisure, and by convention, we treat good x_0^h as leisure. The function $u^h\left(\mathbf{x}^h\right)$ is the utility function of each individual of type h. In the standard utilitarian approach, the social welfare function in (1) satisfies several properties.

2.3.1 Individualism

The utility functions are individualistic in the sense that they represent the preferences of the individual over the commodities consumed. This rules out paternalistic preferences of the government or other institutions overriding those of the individual. Moreover, it does not allow for interdependent utilities, where one individual's utility depends on commodities consumed by another. As discussed in Section 4.2, interdependent utilities raise some difficult conceptual issues that have relevance for tax policy. Note also that social welfare depends on the utility level that individuals reach ex post as a result of policy interventions. It does not depend on where they start out in the absence of the policy.

2.3.2 Pareto Principle

The social welfare function $W(\cdot)$ is generally increasing in each of its arguments, with the exception of the leximin and maximin cases discussed in Section 2.2.3. This is a non-controversial assumption, although it does mean that social welfare increases if, say, the best-off person becomes better off and nobody is made worse off so the allocation of resources is more unequally distributed.

2.3.3 Concavity and Symmetry

The social welfare function $W(\cdot)$ is assumed to be concave and symmetric in individual utilities. Symmetry means that all individuals are given equal weight in the social welfare function, and concavity means that the social welfare function displays a non-decreasing aversion to inequality. To understand this, assume that the social welfare function in (1) takes the symmetric constant-elasticity-of-substitution (CES) form:

$$W(\cdot) = \sum_{h=1}^{H} n^h \frac{u^h(\cdot)^{1-\gamma}}{1-\gamma}, \tag{2}$$

where the parameter γ is the aversion to inequality of the government. To achieve concavity of $W(\cdot)$, we assume $0 \leq \gamma < \infty$ with $\gamma \neq 1$. Differentiating (2), we see that γ is the elasticity of the marginal utility of social welfare with respect to any individual's utility:

$$\gamma = -\frac{1}{u^h} \frac{\mathcal{W}_{u^h u^h}}{\mathcal{W}_{u^h}},$$

where we follow the convention of using subscripts to refer to a partial derivative of a function. The assumption that $\gamma \geq 0$ is equivalent to $\mathcal{W}_{u^h u^h} \leq 0$, as required for concavity.

It is useful to distinguish three cases corresponding to different values of γ. If $\gamma = 0$ so there is no aversion to inequality, (2) takes the linear form: $\mathcal{W}(\cdot) = \sum_h n^h u^h(\cdot)$. This is the *classical utilitarian case* where only the sum of utilities counts and not their distribution. (It is equivalent to the previously mentioned equal marginal sacrifice principle.) In the two-type case ($h = 1, 2$), social indifference curves in utilities u^1 and u^2 are linear and parallel with slopes equal to n^2/n^1. This does not mean that the distribution of income does not count. If the individual utility function is strictly concave in income, social welfare will be higher if a given amount of aggregate income is distributed more evenly.

At the other extreme, suppose $\gamma \to \infty$. In this case, social welfare approaches the *leximin case* where social welfare depends on the utility of the individual with the lowest utility level. Choices between two allocations under leximin are determined as follows. For each allocation, individuals are ranked by their utility levels. The allocation in which the lowest-ranked person has the highest utility level is preferred. If the lowest-ranked persons have identical utility levels, the allocation in which the second-lowest-ranked person has the higher utility level is preferred. If the second-lowest-ranked persons have the same utility, the procedure is repeated for the third lowest and so on until the tie is broken. In the case of two types, social indifference curves under leximin are right-angled along the 45° line.[1] Finally, when $0 < \gamma < \infty$, aversion to inequality is positive and finite and increases with γ.[2] In the two-person case, social indifference curves in u^1 and u^2 are convex to the origin with curvatures that increase as γ increases.

---

[1] Leximin can be contrasted with maximin in which only the least well-off persons are compared. If the least well-off persons have the same utility level in two allocations, the two allocations are socially equivalent under maximin despite the fact that the next least well-off persons might have different levels of utility.

[2] The social welfare function (2) is undefined when $\gamma = 1$. Instead, taking the limit as $\gamma \to 1$, the expression to (2) reduces to $\mathcal{W}(\cdot) = \sum_{h=1}^{H} n^h \ln u^h$, which is the Cobb–Douglas social welfare function.

2.3.4 Measurability, Concavity and Comparability of Utility

Applying the social welfare function in (1) to tax policy analysis requires that individual utility functions be specified and that they be comparable among individuals. There is a literature on the issue of measurability and comparability of utilities, and we can only summarize some key features of it.[3]

Measurability of utility can take various forms. The least demanding is ordinality. Ordinal utility functions are unique up to any positive monotonic transformation, so only preference rankings are possible. If utility levels are comparable across individuals, leximin-type social orderings are possible.[4] Formally, suppose persons a and b obtain utilities $u(x_a)$ and $u(x_b)$ from commodities x_a and x_b. If these are ordinal utility functions, they can be replaced by $\varnothing(u(x_a))$ and $\varnothing(u(x_b))$, where $\varnothing(\cdot)$ is an increasing function and is the same for both persons to satisfy measurability. If $u(x_a) > u(x_b)$, then $\varnothing(u(x_a)) > \varnothing(u(x_b))$, and vice versa, so the ordering of levels of utility are preserved. A social welfare function that relies only on rankings of individual utilities, like maximin or leximin, is permissible since social welfare rankings are not affected by a common monotonic transformation applied to all individuals' utility functions.

Cardinality is a higher degree of measurability. Cardinal utility functions are unique up to a positive affine transformation, which implies that $u(x)$ can be replaced by $v(x) = c + ku(x)$ with $k > 0$. If in addition utility functions are comparable across individuals such that any common affine transformation applies to all of them, a utilitarian social welfare function is possible. To see this, consider the utility functions for a and b above and subject them to a common positive affine transformation, so $v(x_a) = c + ku(x_a)$ and $v(x_b) = c + ku(x_b)$. It follows that

$$v(x_a) \gtreqless v(x_b) \text{ as } u(x_a) \gtreqless u(x_b), \tag{3}$$

$$v(x_a') - v(x_a) \gtreqless v(x_b') - v(x_b) \text{ as } u(x_a') - u(x_a) \gtreqless u(x_b') - u(x_b), \tag{4}$$

where x_a' and x_b' are alternative bundles of commodities for a and b, respectively. The ranking of levels and first differences in utility are unaffected by common positive affine transformations, so both leximin and utilitarian social welfare functions are permissible.

Cardinal individual utility functions are also assumed to be strictly concave, so, for example, they exhibit diminishing marginal utility of income, and this

---

[3] See the survey in Boadway and Bruce (1984), chapter 5.
[4] Leximin social orderings also require an equity axiom to ensure that the least well-off persons are favoured.

concavity is maintained under a positive affine transformation. That is, $v''(x) = ku''(x)$, so if $u(x)$ is strictly concave, so will $v(x)$ be. The concavity of individual utility functions ensures that even if the social welfare function is utilitarian and exhibits zero aversion to utility inequality, the government will pursue policies that redistribute from higher- to lower-income persons.

Greater precision of measurability can lead to more general social welfare functions. For example, suppose utility is strictly concave and unique up to a ratio-scale transformation. Thus, if $u(x)$ is a representation of consumer utility, so is $v(x) = ku(x)$. If utility is also comparable across individuals, social welfare is unique up to a common ratio-scale transformation applied to all individual utility functions. In this case, we obtain

$$\frac{v(x'_a) - v(x_a)}{v(x_a)} \gtreqless \frac{v(x'_b) - v(x_b)}{v(x_b)} \text{ as } \frac{u(x'_a) - u(x_a)}{u(x_a)} \gtreqless \frac{u(x'_b) - u(x_b)}{u(x_b)}.$$

and (3) and (4) continue to apply. Social welfare functions like the CES form in (2) are now permissible.

In the most general case, utility is fully measurable such that utility function transformations cannot be applied. Any general social welfare function (1) becomes admissible.

A judgment must be made about how utility diminishes as consumption rises. There is no objective answer to this, although some maintain that in principle, utility can be measured objectively (e.g., Kaplow, 2008). Usually, some assumption is made that incorporates one's notion of vertical equity. The matter becomes more complicated if individuals differ in their ability to enjoy consumption, for example, because of some disability. Some judgment must be made about how much more weight to give to consumption needs of those who require more consumption to generate given levels of utility. As Sen (1973) observed, this can have real policy consequences. Under a leximin social welfare function, consumption would be redistributed to those less able to enjoy it so that utilities are equalized, while under classical utilitarianism, redistribution would go to those better able to generate utility from consumption so that more total utility is produced.

In what follows, we take as given a general social welfare function of form (1). Unlike in the ability-to-pay and personal expenditure approaches discussed previously, the progressivity of the tax system is determined by the form of the social welfare function and the individual utility functions. We study the optimal income tax problem in more detail below. Before doing so, we discuss some concerns with the social welfare–maximizing approach to tax policy.

2.3.5 Source of Social Welfare Function

A natural question is: Where does the social welfare function come from? It is a normative concept that is meant to capture certain properties that are appealing on ethical grounds. These include individualism and the Pareto principle and also the assumption of non-negative aversion to inequality. Many of the qualitative properties of normative tax policy come from these properties. They may correspond to what comes out of the political process, provided citizens vote according to their social values rather than individual self-interest.

One approach is to suppose that the government's redistributive preferences reflect the collective preferences of citizens. One immediately faces the voting paradox of Arrow (1951), who showed that it is generally impossible to aggregate individual preference orderings into a transitive social ordering. To avoid this, assumptions can be made to ensure that preferences over redistribution are single-peaked. This can be achieved, for example, if the government is restricted to a linear progressive income tax (Gans and Smart, 1996) or if government decision-making is entrusted to a single authority, the *citizen-candidate* (Osborne and Slivinski, 1996).

Another approach is to assume that redistribution is motivated by the altruism of the rich (Hochman and Rodgers, 1969). In this case, redistribution is based on efficiency, but because voluntary transfers of the rich are constrained by free-riding behaviour, the government redistributes on their behalf. The drawback of this approach is that only the utility of the rich matters for redistribution, albeit utility that includes the altruistic benefit the rich get from the well-being of the poor. The altruistic approach leads to less redistribution than social welfare maximization would propose. It could also affect the form of redistribution if the rich have preferences over the way the poor spend their income (e.g., in-kind transfers of goods). This would be inconsistent with transfers to the poor motivated by social welfare maximization, where the arguments of the social welfare function are utility levels as judged by individuals themselves.

Regardless of its source, the social welfare function represents a normative social ordering that can be used as a standard against which to judge existing policies and recommend alternatives. We return below to empirical studies of the basis for social welfare functions.

2.3.6 Relevance of Pre-tax Position

A criticism of the utilitarian approach expressed by Feldstein (2012) and mentioned previously is that optimal tax policy is based only on individuals' well-being with taxes in place. No account is taken of pre-tax positions. To put it another way, initial positions reflect property held by individuals, including their skills, and optimal tax theory gives no weight to ownership rights to that property.

From the point of view of utilitarian theory, the government treats individual skills as public property whose fruits can be redistributed to satisfy utilitarian objectives. Indeed, in a world of full information, optimal income taxation reduces to optimal redistribution based on observable skills, which to those like Feldstein represents confiscation of property rights. For that reason, some have referred to redistribution as akin to theft or coercion (Martinez-Vazquez and Winer, 2014). Giving at least partial ownership rights over human skills to individuals would limit the extent of redistribution.

3 Policy Implications from Optimal Tax Theory

This section summarizes the main policy-relevant results from optimal tax theory. The optimal tax literature studies revenue-raising and redistribution from a normative perspective. The government maximizes a social welfare function that satisfies specified ethical properties. It can be contrasted with positive approaches to taxation that seek to explain how the political process determines government tax-transfer policy. The literature on optimal taxation is vast and has grown rapidly in recent years. Our purpose here is to provide a broad overview of the literature and its implications for tax policy.

We first discuss the representative-agent model due to Ramsey (1927) that focuses on efficiency considerations and establishes the methodological approach. We then turn to two standard models of optimal redistributive taxation, which differ in their treatment of labour supply. In the *intensive-margin model* originating in Mirrlees (1971), individuals adjust the intensity of their labour supply in response to after-tax wages and incomes. In the *extensive-margin model* of Diamond (1980), individuals make discrete labour supply decisions such as labour market participation and job choice. These models share some common features, including a given distribution of workers by skill or productivity levels, a perfectly elastic demand for labour and common social welfare functions. They also emphasize information as a basic constraint on the government achieving its redistributive objectives. We outline the tax-transfer structures obtained from these two approaches and stress their policy-relevant features, including those obtained from simulations.

3.1 Optimal Taxation of the Representative Individual

The seminal paper by Ramsey (1927) sets out the basic optimal tax methodology. It focuses on a representative price-taking individual who obtains utility from m commodities, each of which is subject to a commodity tax. Lump-sum taxes are ruled out. Ramsey studies how to obtain a given amount of revenue from the individual with the least loss in utility. Subsequent analyses by

Samuelson (1986) and Diamond and Mirrlees (1971) have formulated the Ramsey problem as follows. Suppose there are $m + 1$ commodities, denoted by i, $i = 0, \ldots, m$, where commodities 1 to m are goods with consumer prices $q = q_1, \ldots, q_m$ and commodity zero is leisure with price w. Letting leisure be the numeraire with $w = 1$, indirect utility is $v(q)$, where consumer prices for the m goods are $q_i = p_i + t_i$ for commodity taxes t_i and producer prices p_i. Leisure is not taxed. (Producer prices are fixed for simplicity.) The government maximizes $v(q)$ subject to a revenue constraint $\sum_i t_i x_i = R$, and the first-order conditions yield the following:[5]

$$\sum_{i=1}^{m} t_i \frac{\partial x_i}{\partial q_k} = -\left(\frac{\lambda - \alpha}{\lambda}\right) x_k \quad k = 1, \ldots, m, \tag{5}$$

where λ is the Lagrange multiplier on government revenue and α is the individual's marginal utility of consumption, with $\lambda > \alpha$. Equation (5) is surprisingly complex for a seemingly simple problem and does not lead to straightforward interpretations. Some special cases provide intuition for policy purposes.

3.1.1 Inverse Elasticity Rule

Assume utility is quasi-linear in leisure and additive, so takes the form $u(x) = x_0 + u_1(x_1) + \ldots + u_m(x_m)$. The demand functions for the m goods take the partial elasticity form, $x_i(q_i)$, and (5) becomes:[6]

$$\tau_k \equiv \frac{t_k}{q_k} = -\left(\frac{\lambda - \alpha}{\lambda}\right) \frac{1}{\eta_{kk}} \quad k = 1, \ldots, m, \tag{6}$$

where η_{kk} is the own-price elasticity of demand for good x_k. Optimal ad valorem tax rates on each good are inversely proportional to the elasticity of demand.

3.1.2 Proportionate Reduction Rule

Rewrite (6):

$$\frac{t_k}{x_k} \frac{\partial x_k}{\partial q_k} = \frac{\Delta q_k}{x_k} \frac{\partial x_k}{\partial \hat{q}_k} \cong \frac{\Delta x_k}{x_k} = -\left(\frac{\lambda - \alpha}{\lambda}\right) \quad k = 1, \ldots, m.$$

---

[5] To derive (5), we have used $\partial v / \partial q_i = -\alpha x_i$, which follows from the individual's utility maximization problem. The Lagrangian for this problem is $\mathcal{L} = u(x) - \alpha \sum_i q_i x_i$. The solution yields demand functions $x_i(q)$ and the indirect utility function $v(q) \equiv u\big(x(q)\big)$. The envelope theorem says $\partial v(q) / \partial q_i = \partial \mathcal{L} / \partial q_i = -\alpha x_i$.

[6] Maximizing $u(x) = x_0 + u_1(x_1) + \ldots + u_m(x_m)$ subject to $\sum_i q_i x_i = 0$ gives the first-order conditions $\partial u_i(x_i) / \partial x_i = \alpha q_i$, whose solutions yield $x_i(q_i)$.

Optimal commodity taxes cause the demand for all goods to fall proportionately.

3.1.3 Ramsey Rule

Substituting the Slutsky equation into (5) and using the symmetry of the substitution effect, we obtain[7]

$$\frac{\sum_i t_i s_{ki}}{x_k} = -\left(\frac{\lambda - \alpha}{\lambda}\right) + \sum_i t_i \frac{\partial x_i}{\partial y} = -(1 - \beta) \quad k = 1, \ldots, m, \tag{7}$$

where s_{ki} is the substitution effect of a change in q_i on the compensated demand for x_k and $\beta = \alpha/\lambda + \sum t_i \partial x_i / \partial y$ is the net social marginal utility of income. This is referred to as the Ramsey rule by Samuelson (1986) and Diamond and Mirrlees (1971), although it differs from the version of the optimal tax rule that Ramsey actually derived. It says that optimal taxes should cause an equal proportionate reduction in the demand for all commodities if the individual is compensated to remain on the same indifference curve. As Diamond and Mirrlees showed, this rule still applies even if producer prices are not fixed. Thus, only demand elasticities are relevant, and not supply elasticities.

3.1.4 The Corlett–Hague Theorem

One of the most influential results in optimal commodity taxation is the *Corlett–Hague theorem* based on a tax reform analysis found in Corlett and Hague (1953) and extrapolated to an optimal tax result in Harberger (1964) and Diamond and Mirrlees (1971). Corlett and Hague used a setting with two goods and leisure and analyzed a revenue-neutral differential commodity tax reform starting from uniform commodity taxes on the two goods.

In the context of the above model, rewrite (7) for $k = 1, 2$ as follows:

$$t_1 s_{11} + t_2 s_{12} = -(1 - \beta)x_1; \quad t_1 s_{21} + t_2 s_{22} = -(1 - \beta)x_2.$$

Combining these two expressions, we obtain

$$\frac{t_1/q_1}{t_2/q_2} = \frac{\tau_1}{\tau_2} = \frac{\varepsilon_{22} - \varepsilon_{12}}{\varepsilon_{11} - \varepsilon_{21}} = \frac{\varepsilon_{22} + \varepsilon_{11} + \varepsilon_{10}}{\varepsilon_{11} + \varepsilon_{22} + \varepsilon_{20}}, \tag{8}$$

---

[7] The Slutsky equation decomposes the effect of a change in q_j on the uncompensated demand for good i, $x_i(q)$, into a substitution and an income effect: $\partial x_i/\partial q_j = \partial \tilde{x}_i/\partial q_j - x_j \partial x_i/\partial y = s_{ij} - x_j \partial x_i/\partial y$, where $\tilde{x}_i$ is the compensated demand for good i, y is income, and the substitution effect s_{ij} is symmetric so $s_{ij} = s_{ji}$.

where ε_{ij} is the compensated elasticity of demand for x_i with respect to q_i and the last equality follows from the compensated demands for any good being homogeneous of degree zero, $\sum_i \varepsilon_{ij} = 0$. This is the Corlett–Hague theorem and implies $\tau_1 \gtrless \tau_2$ as $\varepsilon_{20} \gtrless \varepsilon_{10}$. That is, the tax rate should be higher on the good that is relatively more complementary with leisure, x_0. The intuition is that since leisure is untaxed, a tax reform that indirectly taxes leisure would be welfare-improving.

This result is invoked in various tax policy issues, such as the tax treatment of present versus future consumption, or equivalently, capital income taxation. An analogous argument for taxing goods that are complementary with leisure also appears in an optimal non-linear income tax context as discussed later.

3.1.5 Uniform Commodity Taxes

A natural extension of the Corlett–Hague theorem involves the circumstances under which uniform commodity taxes, or a labour income tax, is optimal. By (8), taxes should be proportional if $\varepsilon_{10} = \varepsilon_{20}$, so both goods are equally complementary with leisure. This readily generalizes to the case of m goods plus leisure. If $t_i/q_i = \tau$ for all goods $i = 1, \ldots, m$, (7) gives

$$\frac{\sum_i t_i s_{ki}}{x_k} = \frac{\tau \left(\sum_i s_{ki} q_i \right)}{x_k} = \tau \sum_{i=1}^{m} \varepsilon_{ki} = -(1 - \beta), \quad k = 1, \ldots, m.$$

By homogeneity of compensated demands, $\sum_{i=0}^{m} \varepsilon_{ki} = 0$. Therefore, $\tau \varepsilon_{k0} = (1 - \beta)$ for all m goods, or $\varepsilon_{k0} = \varepsilon_{j0}$ for all j, k. That is, all goods must be equally substitutable with leisure.

As discussed in Sandmo (1976), a sufficient condition for this is that the utility function is weakly separable, $u(f(x_1, \ldots, x_m), x_0)$, with $f(\cdot)$ homothetic.[8] In this case, the income elasticity of all m goods is unity. A proportional tax on all goods reduces all demands proportionately, so the proportionate reduction rule is satisfied and the tax is optimal. Weak separability and homotheticity are strong requirements and unlikely to be satisfied in practice. However, as we shall see, as the optimal tax problem becomes more general and the government's policy instruments broader, conditions for uniformity of commodity taxes become less demanding. This is of policy relevance since uniform taxes are much easier to apply and less costly to administer. For example, broad-based VAT systems approximate a uniform consumption tax.

---

[8] The function $f(\cdot)$ is homothetic if the marginal rate of substitution between any pair of goods x_i and x_j is constant along a ray through the origin in (x_i, x_j)-space or equivalently depends only on the ratio of the two goods, x_j/x_i. If $f(\cdot)$ is homogeneous of any degree k, it will be homothetic.

3.2 Optimal Taxation of Heterogeneous Individuals

We review the two classic approaches to optimal income taxation associated with Mirrlees (1971) and Diamond (1980). In both approaches, individuals differ in an innate characteristic called productivity that determines the income they are able to earn. In the Mirrlees approach, individuals have the same preferences for goods and labour (or leisure). They can vary the intensity with which they supply labour that together with their productivity determines their income. The government cannot observe productivity or wage rates, which individuals cannot influence, but can observe incomes. With perfect information, the government could condition individual lump-sum transfers and taxes on productivity and achieve any feasible distribution of income without any efficiency losses. In contrast, if the government can observe only incomes, individuals can choose their incomes to partially frustrate the government's desire to redistribute income. Formally, the government faces an incentive constraint that precludes it from redistributing income so much that higher productivity individuals prefer to choose incomes corresponding with those of lesser productivity.

Diamond instead assumes that hours of work are fixed and individuals can choose only to work or not. Individual income is now determined by the individual's innate productivity and their work participation decision. Individuals differ in their preferences for non-participation, and the government cannot observe those preferences. If the government imposes a higher tax on individuals of a given income, some of them will choose not to participate and that constitutes inefficiency caused by income taxation. In both the Mirrlees intensive-margin approach and the Diamond extensive-margin approach, individuals face perfectly elastic demands for their labour, so wage rates are fixed and any labour supplied finds employment.

The government chooses a tax structure to maximize a social welfare function that captures society's equity values. It may be limited in the form of tax function it can use, for example, linear progressive versus non-linear. In both approaches, optimal taxes trade off efficiency versus equity concerns and take into consideration the distribution of skills, individual preferences and the form of the social welfare function. We consider the intensive- and extensive-margin approaches in turn.

3.2.1 Intensive-Margin Labour Supply Approach

Following Mirrlees (1971), the economy is populated by individuals who differ in their given productivity, which is reflected in their wage rate w. Wages are distributed by a distribution function $F(w)$ on $[\underline{w}, \overline{w}]$ with $\underline{w} \geq 0$ and density

$f(w)$. The population is normalized to unity, so $F(\overline{w}) = 1$. Individuals of type w choose labour supply and earn an income of $y(w) = w\ell(w)$ also referred to as their *effective labour supply*. They pay taxes according to the income tax function $T(y)$, leaving $c(w) = y(w) - T(y(w))$ as consumption. In the Mirrlees model, consumption is aggregated into a single composite commodity. When we consider commodity taxes, a disaggregated approach will be taken. All individuals have the same utility function $u(c, \ell)$, which is increasing in c, decreasing in ℓ and strictly concave and implies utility is fully measurable.

Production in the economy is particularly simple. Output is linear in effective labour supplied, so the total output is $Y = \int_{\underline{w}}^{\overline{w}} w\ell(w)f(w)dw$. This implies that the demand for labour is perfectly elastic: if a type$-w$ individual increases labour supply, the additional labour supplied will be employed at the wage w. This in turn implies that all responses to taxation come from the labour supply changes. We return to alternative labour demand environments later.

The government chooses its tax function to maximize an additive social welfare function based on a vector of individual utilities $\boldsymbol{u}(\cdot)$:

$$\mathcal{W}\Big(\boldsymbol{u}(\cdot)f(\boldsymbol{w})\Big) = \int_{\underline{w}}^{\overline{w}} W\Big(u\big(c(w), \ell(w)\big)\Big)f(w)dw$$

$$= \int_{\underline{w}}^{\overline{w}} W\Big(u\big(c(w), \frac{y(w)}{w}\big)\Big)f(w)dw, \tag{9}$$

where $W(u(c(w), \ell(w)))$ is a social utility function applying to each individual and is increasing in utility and concave and $\mathcal{W}(\boldsymbol{u}(\cdot)f(\boldsymbol{w}))$ is symmetric in individual utilities. The assumption of concavity implies that the government has a non-negative aversion to utility inequality. If social utility $W(u(\cdot))$ is strictly concave, marginal social utility $W'(u(\cdot))$ will be decreasing in individual utility. A redistribution of income from high- to low-utility persons increases social welfare. The degree of concavity of the social welfare function represents the weight put on equity by the government, that is, the *aversion to utility inequality*. It corresponds with the parameter γ in the previously given CES social welfare function (2). In the *utilitarian* case, the social utility function is linear, and social welfare is linear in individuals' utilities. Since individual utilities are strictly concave in income, the government will want to redistribute income from high- to low-income persons. The extreme case of inequality aversion is the *maximin* case where the government only cares about the lowest-utility person. The government also faces a budget constraint of the form:

$$\int_{\underline{w}}^{\overline{w}} T\Big(y(w)\Big)f(w)dw = R, \qquad (10)$$

where $R \geq 0$ is the revenue required to finance given government expenditures.

We distinguish between two forms of the government income tax function $T(y)$. In the first case, $T(y)$ is *linear progressive* so consists of a constant marginal tax rate and a fixed tax credit for which all taxpayers are eligible. In the second case, the optimal income tax function is *non-linear*. In both cases, we assume that the government can observe individuals' incomes, but not their labour supplies or their wage rates. This assumption is motivated by the fact that in actual tax systems, individuals report their incomes to the tax authority. We assume that they do so truthfully. This is a strong assumption and requires that the tax administration can enforce truthful reporting by its system of audits and penalties.

We begin with the simpler case of redistributive linear income taxes and then consider non-linear income taxes.

3.2.2 Linear Progressive Income Taxation

Following Sheshinski (1972), suppose the government is restricted to a linear progressive income tax, $T(y) = ty - b$, where t is the marginal tax rate and b is an equal lump-sum transfer to all individuals. To facilitate the government's problem, individual utility is written in the indirect form as a function of the tax parameters (t, b), where the indirect utility function is as follows:

$$v(t, b; w) \equiv \max_{\{c, \ell\}} \quad u(c, \ell) \quad \text{s.t.} \quad c = (1 - t)w\ell + b. \qquad (11)$$

The indirect utility function is useful for analyzing tax policy because it takes into account individual behavioural responses to tax changes. The value of the Lagrange multiplier on the budget constraint in problem (11) is the *marginal utility of income* and given the linear progressive tax system is equivalent to $\partial v(t, b; w)/\partial b$. Indirect utility is increasing in wages, and the marginal utility of income is non-increasing in wages. Higher-wage individuals value an additional dollar in after-tax income less than lower-wage individuals.

The problem of the government is to maximize a social welfare function subject to a budget constraint with a revenue requirement R, or

$$\max_{\{t,b\}} \int_{\underline{w}}^{\overline{w}} W(v(t,b;w)) f(w)dw \quad \text{s.t.} \quad \int_{\underline{w}}^{\overline{w}} tw\ell(t,b;w)f(w)dw = b + R, \qquad (12)$$

where $b = \int_{\underline{w}}^{\overline{w}} bf(w)dw$ since population size is normalized to unity. The solution to this problem yields optimal values of b and t.

To facilitate the interpretation of the solution to this problem, it is useful to introduce two definitions. One is the *marginal social utility of income* for a type$-w$ individual, which is the change in social welfare from an increase in the after-tax income or consumption of a type$-w$ person:

$$\alpha(w) \equiv \frac{\partial W\Big(v(t,b;w)\Big)}{\partial v(t,b;w)} \cdot \frac{\partial v(t,b;w)}{\partial b}. \qquad (13)$$

The marginal social utility of income is the product of two terms. The first is the change in social welfare from an increase in type$-w$'s utility. The second is type$-w$'s marginal utility of income as previously defined. Since the social utility function is concave and individual utilities are strictly concave, $\alpha(w)$ is decreasing in w: an increment of after-tax income is more socially valuable for lower-wage persons. The marginal social utility of income is defined for a given tax rate.

Next, the *net social marginal value of income* extends $\beta(w)$ by taking account of the fact that giving an increment of after-tax income to an individual has indirect effects on government revenue by changing the amount of income the individual will earn. It is evaluated in terms of government revenue and is defined as follows:

$$\beta(w) \equiv \frac{\alpha(w)}{\lambda} + \frac{\partial y(t,b;w)}{\partial b}, \qquad (14)$$

where λ is the value of the Lagrange multiplier on the government revenue constraint in (12). The second term in (14) represents an indirect revenue effect arising from the behavioural response of the individual to an increase in non-labour income. Assuming leisure is normal, this second term is negative and larger for higher$-w$ persons. Then, $\beta(w)$ will also be decreasing in w.

Armed with these definitions, the first-order conditions to the government's problem for t and b yield the following result:[9]

---

[9] In what follows, we do not write out the first-order conditions of the government explicitly. The optimal tax expressions we state can be derived from them in a straightforward way.

$$\frac{t}{1-t} = -\frac{\int_{\underline{w}}^{\overline{w}} \left(\beta(w) - 1\right) w \ell f(w) dw}{\int_{\underline{w}}^{\overline{w}} w \ell \epsilon_\ell f(w) dw} = -\frac{\text{Cov}[\beta, y]}{\int_{\underline{w}}^{\overline{w}} y \epsilon_\ell f(w) dw} = \frac{\text{equity}}{\text{efficiency}},$$

(15)

$$\mathbb{E}[\beta] = 1,$$

(16)

where ϵ_ℓ is the compensated elasticity of labour supply with respect to the after-tax wage rate and $y = w\ell$. The optimal tax rate is determined by (15), which is the ratio of equity and an efficiency effect. The tax rate is inversely related to an aggregate of compensated elasticities of labour supply weighted by total incomes at each wage level. This is the distortionary or efficiency effect of the income tax. The tax rate is increasing in the covariance of the net social marginal value of income with income. The more rapidly $\beta(w)$ declines with w (i.e., the greater the concavity of the social and individual utility functions), and the more dispersed is income, the higher the tax rate. Equation (15) reflects the equity–efficiency trade-off in choosing the tax rate and will be a useful basis for comparison with later results.

The optimal lump-sum transfer b satisfies (16). The left-hand side represents the average net social marginal benefit of an incremental increase in b, and the right-hand side represents the marginal cost of this increase (since the population is normalized to one). In the optimum, these two are equal. As (15) and (16) indicate, the optimal values of t and b depend on the underlying wage distribution, the compensated elasticity of labour supply, the revenue requirement and the social welfare function.

Without income effects and assuming a constant elasticity of labour supply, Tanninen et al. (2019) show analytically that with an unbounded Pareto wage distribution and a constant aversion-to-utility-inequality social welfare function, the optimal t and b are both increasing in the degree of aversion to utility inequality. They also show that the more revenue is required, the higher is the tax rate t, but less of the tax revenue is available for the lump-sum transfer, and therefore, the lower is optimal b.

With a maximin social welfare function, the government maximizes the welfare of the lowest-utility person, who is the one with the lowest wage rate, $\underline{w}$, so $\alpha(w) = 0$ for all $w > \underline{w}$. This case also yields the largest feasible lump-sum transfer b, when the government is restricted to a linear progressive income tax. Suppose for simplicity that $\underline{w} = 0$ so the lowest-wage person earns no income. Then, the welfare of the least well-off person is maximized when the government chooses t to maximize b from the government budget constraint in (12). This yields the *tax-revenue maximizing tax rate* given by (16) with $\beta(w) = t\partial y(t, b; w)/\partial b$ for all $w > \underline{w}$. Without income effects and if all individuals have the same constant compensated elasticity of labour supply ϵ, the maximin optimal tax rate is $t/(1 - t) = 1/\epsilon$, which is less than one. The government is constrained in its ability to raise tax revenue only by the behavioural responses of individuals. Provided the lowest-wage individuals are not working, the government does not need to be concerned about how the tax rate affects these individuals since they are not paying any income taxes.

If $\underline{w} > 0$ and $y(\underline{w}) > 0$, then a government with a maximin objective must take into account how the tax rate impacts the lowest-wage individuals. The optimal tax rate with no income effects and constant elasticity will be

$$\frac{t}{1 - t} = \frac{1}{\epsilon}\left(1 - \frac{y(\underline{w})}{\mathbb{E}[y]}\right),$$

where the term in the brackets reflects the equity concerns for the lowest-wage individuals and will necessarily be less than one so the optimal tax rate will be lower than the tax revenue–maximizing rate. The higher the income of the lowest-wage individuals relative to the average income, the lower the optimal tax rate.

3.2.3 Optimal Commodity Taxes

Suppose now each good has its own indirect tax rate. As stated previously, there are m goods, $x = (x_1, \ldots, x_i, \ldots, x_m)$, and write utility as $u(x, \ell)$. The government can now impose a linear progressive income tax with parameters t and b and commodity taxes τ_i on goods $i = 1, \ldots, m$. If quantities of goods are measured such that producer prices equal unity, the individual's budget constraint can be written as follows:

$$\sum_{i=1}^{m}(1 + \tau_i)x_i = (1 - t)y + b.$$

It would be welfare-improving to deploy commodity taxes only if it is optimal to impose differential tax rates. If optimal commodity taxes are uniform, commodity taxes are redundant since their effect can be subsumed into the income tax system.

Deaton (1979) showed that if the government is restricted to a linear progressive income tax, commodity taxes should not be differentiated if individual preferences are (a) weakly separable in commodities and leisure and (b) quasi-homothetic in commodities (i.e., homothetic to some point). That is, Engel curves for all goods are linear and of the same slope for all individuals.[10] (Recall

---

[10] An Engel curve shows how the demand for good i varies with income holding all prices constant.

that for the representative-individual case, homotheticity of the sub-utility function is sufficient for optimal taxes to be uniform, which is a stronger condition.) An example of a quasi-homothetic utility function is the Stone–Geary function, $u(\varphi(x_1 - \bar{x}_1, \ldots, x_i - \bar{x}_i, \ldots, x_m - \bar{x}_m), x_0)$, with $\bar{x}_i$ fixed for all i and $\varphi(\ldots)$ homothetic in its arguments. If the Deaton conditions are satisfied, the optimal tax system is a linear progressive income tax. Deaton also shows that if there is a subset of goods for which Engel curves are linear, commodity taxes within the group should be uniform.

To put the Deaton conditions into context, recall the inverse elasticity rule of the representative-individual case. Goods, like necessities, that have low-price elasticities of demand tend to have low-income elasticities of demand, and the opposite for luxuries. While efficiency considerations suggest higher taxes on necessities, equity considerations do the opposite, leading to an equity–efficiency trade-off. When the Deaton conditions are satisfied, equity and efficiency forces are exactly offsetting.

The policy relevance of the Deaton conditions has been enhanced by an insight from Hellwig (2009, 2010). Suppose there is a non-optimal tax system consisting of a linear progressive income tax and a set of differentiated commodity taxes. Hellwig showed that if the Deaton conditions are satisfied, a Pareto-improving tax reform could be implemented consisting of a move to a uniform commodity tax system and a suitable change in the parameters of the income tax. The elimination of differential commodity taxes removes a distortion that affects all individuals, while the change in income tax parameters addresses any equity consequences. This Pareto-improving tax reform result is significant because it does not involve an equity–efficiency trade-off. Moreover, it applies even if the linear progressive income tax is not optimal. In fact, if the reform leaves the income tax parameters t and b at non-optimal values, social welfare could naturally be improved by moving to the optimum. However, unlike the Hellwig reform, this would not necessarily be Pareto-improving.

3.2.4 Production Efficiency

Much of the optimal tax literature neglects the production side of the economy by assuming that production possibilities are linear and producer prices are fixed. Moreover, taxes are usually specified as applying to individuals directly or on sales of final goods to individuals. In the real world, taxes also apply on the transactions of firms. Commodity taxes may apply to purchases of intermediate inputs by firms, and differential taxes may apply on firms' uses of primary inputs like labour and capital. For example, the corporate tax applies selectively to capital income generated in the corporate sector, and payroll taxes on labour may differ by firm characteristics such as size. As well, small firms may escape taxation altogether either because they operate informally or because there is a threshold size for liability to collect VATs. Taxes on intermediate inputs and differential taxes on capital or labour cause production inefficiencies, and the economy will be operating inside its production possibilities frontier.

Diamond and Mirrlees (1971) show that when taxes are chosen optimally and all pure profits (rents) are fully taxed, production efficiency should apply. The argument is relatively simple. Suppose there are a number of producers in the economy indexed by k. Let s^k be producer k's production vector and assume it taken from the producer's feasible production set S^k. The resource constraint for the economy can be written as $\sum_k x^j + g = \sum s^k \in \sum_k S^k$, where g is net government production. The government maximizes social welfare $W(v^1(q), \ldots, v^H(q))$ subject to the resource constraint, where q is the set of consumer prices facing all individuals. Suppose aggregate production $\sum s^k$ lies in the interior of the aggregate production set $\sum S^k$. The government can choose q independently of p since $q - p = t$. If the government reduces q_i for some good that has a positive net demand by consumers, social welfare will rise, and the increase of production is feasible since we are in the interior of the production set. Thus, in an optimum, $\sum s^k$ must be on the boundary of $\sum S^k$. Intuitively, with production inefficiency, a reduction in the consumer price of a good consumed increases utility, and the increased demand can be satisfied without sacrificing the production of other goods.

The taxation of pure profits is an important assumption in the production efficiency theorem. Any untaxed profits enter into individuals' indirect utility function. Since they depend on prices, there is no guarantee that the reduction in the price of a commodity that individuals demand will be welfare-improving since their share of the profits might fall. The theorem also depends on all goods being taxed. Newbery (1986) shows that if only a subset of commodities is taxed, it may improve welfare to apply a tax on the production of untaxed commodities, which would violate production efficiency.

The production efficiency theorem has two significant policy implications. One is that a VAT is the preferred choice of an indirect commodity tax system. As discussed in Christiansen and Smith (2021), a VAT administered using the input credit method taxes all sales (including imports, but excluding exports) and offers an input tax credit for taxes paid on intermediate purchases. This ensures that there are no effective taxes paid on intermediate inputs, which is necessary for production efficiency. Single-stage commodity taxes cannot avoid taxes being charged on at least some intermediate inputs.

The second is that firms' profits must be fully taxed for production efficiency to apply. The preferred business tax system is one whose base is economic rents or its equivalent. Equivalent systems can include a cash-flow tax and an allow-ance for corporate equity tax (Auerbach et al., 2010). Standard corporate tax systems apply to shareholder income, which is implicitly a tax on capital and leads to production inefficiency. The alternative of no tax at all will lead to an optimal tax system that violates production efficiency as already mentioned.

Note that these arguments for production efficiency also apply when the government can levy a non-linear personal income tax to which we now turn.

3.2.5 Non-linear Income Taxation

Suppose now that the government can levy a non-linear direct tax on individuals. We begin with the standard model of optimal income tax due to Mirrlees, which suppresses commodity taxes, and then we consider a variety of extensions.

The government implements a non-linear income tax $T(y)$, so a type$-w$ individual's budget constraint is $c(w) = y(w) - T(y(w))$. In the standard optimal income tax analysis, the government chooses $y(w)(= w\ell(w))$ and $c(w)$ to maximize social welfare $\mathcal{W}(\cdot)$ subject to a budget constraint and an incentive-compatibility constraint. The latter requires that the government choice of $c(w)$ and $y(w)$ for a type$-w$ individual be consistent with the individual's most preferred bundle. In particular, individual w must prefer the bundle $(c(w), y(w))$ over the bundle intended for any another type w', $(c(w'), y(w'))$. Formally, let a type$-w$'s utility be $u(w) \equiv v(c(w), y(w), w)$. Then, incentive compatibility requires that $u(w) = v(c(w), y(w), w) \geq v(c(w'), y(w'), w) \ \forall w' \neq w$, or $u(w) = \max_{w'} v(c(w'), y(w'), w)$. Applying the envelope theorem to this problem, we obtain the incentive compatibility constraint in the government's problem:[11]

$$\frac{du(w)}{dw} = v_w(c(w), y(w), w). \tag{17}$$

Thus, the government chooses $y(w)$ and $c(w)$ to maximize (9) subject to incentive-compatibility conditions (17) for each individual type and the budget constraint (10). The structure of $T(y(w))$ is inferred from the first-order conditions to the government's problem. The analysis is technical, and in what follows to characterize the optimal tax rules, we instead use a perturbation approach following Saez (2001). This allows us to express the optimal income tax in terms of the income distribution rather than the wage distribution, where

---

[11] Technically, this is the first-order incentive compatibility condition. A second-order incentive compatibility condition must also be satisfied that ensures that the allocation satisfying the first-order incentive compatibility condition is a global maximum. We assume that the condition is satisfied.

the former is observable and more informative for interpreting optimal tax rules for policy purposes.

Following Diamond (1998), assume that individual utility is quasilinear in consumption, and assume a constant elasticity in labour, so utility takes the form:

$$u(c, \ell) = c - \frac{\ell^{1+1/\epsilon}}{1 + 1/\epsilon}, \tag{18}$$

where ϵ is both the compensated and uncompensated elasticity of labour supply given there are no income effects on labour supply.[12] Let the distribution of income in the optimum be $H(y)$ with density $h(y)$,[13] and the tax function in terms of income is $T(y)$. Replacing $\ell = y/w$ in (18) and maximizing subject to the budget constraint $c = y - T(y)$ yields:

$$y = (1 - T'(y))^{\epsilon} w^{1+\epsilon}.$$

So ϵ is also the elasticity of y with respect to $1 - T'(y)$, referred to as the *elasticity of taxable income*.[14] Finally, let $G(y)$ be the average social value in terms of government revenue of giving one unit of income to all persons with income above y:[15]

$$G(y) = \frac{\int_y^{\bar{y}} \left(W'(\tilde{y})/\lambda \right) dH(\tilde{y})}{1 - H(y)}.$$

Since marginal social utility $W'(y)$ is decreasing in y, $G(y)$ will be decreasing in y.

Assume the optimal income tax is in place and consider the following perturbation. Increase the marginal tax rate $T'(y)$ by $dT'(y)$ over the interval $y + dy$, holding $T'(y)$ at all other income levels constant. This perturbation will have the following effects. Those below income level y will not be affected. For those above y, tax liabilities will increase by a lump-sum amount $dT'(y)$ since all such persons at that level will pay more income taxes on their inframarginal income. Their before-tax income will not change since utility is quasilinear, and the increase in government revenue will be $dR = (1 - H(y))dT'(y)$ because

---

[12] The following results could easily be generalized to allow for the elasticity of labour supply to depend on the individual's underlying wage rate or equivalently, income.

[13] If income, $y = w\ell$, is increasing in w, the distributions of wages and incomes satisfy $H(y) = F(w)$ and $f(w) = h(y)dy/dw$.

[14] In Saez et al. (2012), the elasticity of taxable income refers more generally to when individuals can vary their income by other actions besides changing labour supply. Examples include tax avoidance and evasion, postponing tax liabilities, and changing the form in which income is earned when different forms face different tax rates.

[15] Social welfare continues to be defined as an additive social welfare function that is increasing and concave in individual utilities where utility is now defined as a function of income, and the aggregation is over the income distribution.

there are $1 - H(y)$ individuals with income greater than y. The loss in social welfare for these individuals will be $dW = -G(y)dR$. For those in the interval $y + dy$, of whom there are $h(y)$, the change in income using the elasticity ϵ is

$$h(y)dy = -\frac{\epsilon h(y)ydT'(y)}{1 - T'(y)},$$

so tax revenue falls by $dB = T'(y)h(y)dy$, or

$$dB = -\frac{\epsilon ydT'(y)}{1 - T'(y)}h(y)T'(y).$$

There is no change in utility of persons in this interval since they are only marginally affected by the tax rate change. Since the economy is initially in an optimum, the sum of these changes is zero, that is, $dR + dW + dB = 0$. Rearranging this, we obtain

$$\frac{T'(y)}{1 - T'(y)} = -\frac{\left(1 - H(y)\right)\left(1 - G(y)\right)}{\epsilon yh(y)} = \frac{\text{equity}}{\text{efficiency}}. \tag{19}$$

As in the linear progressive tax case of (15), the optimal marginal tax rate is inversely related to the elasticity of taxable income multiplied by the total amount of taxable income at income level y (the efficiency effect). It reflects the reduction in the tax base as a result of an increase in the marginal tax rate at income y. The equity term reflects the effect on social welfare of an increase in the marginal tax rate. An increase in $T'(y)$ causes tax liabilities to rise by an equal lump-sum amount for all individuals with incomes above y. The equity term involves the net benefit of transferring tax revenues from the $1 - H(y)$ persons above income level y to the government, where $1 - G(y)$ is the per capita benefit of such a transfer. The equity term can rise or fall with y: the per capita benefit increases with y, but the number of persons facing the higher lump-sum tax depends on the income distribution. Therefore, while $T'(y)$ is non-negative, it can rise or fall with y so can take on many different patterns depending on the underlying wage distribution and assumed social welfare function.[16]

---

[16] Some special cases have been found in the literature, where the focus is on the shape of the optimal marginal income tax schedule in terms of the underlying wage distribution. Diamond (1998) studied the quasilinear case as above and also assumed that the wage distribution was unbounded at the top (i.e., $\overline{w} \to \infty$). If the distribution of w above the median is Pareto, $T'(w)$ will be U-shaped above the median. On the other hand, if $\overline{w}$ is finite, the marginal tax rate falls to zero at the top. Boadway et al. (2000a) show that the Diamond result can also apply when preferences are quasilinear in labour and the social welfare function is utilitarian, but only if the wage distribution is unbounded.

This has been borne out in various numerical simulations that assume different wage distributions, for example, lognormal (Mirrlees, 1971), Pareto (Saez, 2001) and Champernowne (Tuomala, 2016). In all cases, the simulated patterns of the optimal marginal tax rates are affected by the assumed wage distribution, individual preferences and social welfare function.

The optimal marginal tax rate at the bottom and top of the income distribution will both be zero since the equity term in (19) goes to zero at $y = \underline{y}$ and $y = \bar{y}$.[17] The optimal marginal tax rate in the interior must be between zero and one. The significance of the zero marginal tax rate at the top can be discounted since it applies only at the very top, and not immediately below the top. Moreover, the average tax rate at the top can be large even if the marginal tax rate is low.

At the bottom, the zero marginal tax rate is also of limited relevance. If there is bunching at the bottom, so many wage types select the same bundle of y and c (e.g., $y = 0$), the marginal tax rate will be positive. To see this, suppose that the lowest-wage individual supplies zero labour and receives $T(0)$ in consumption. Furthermore, suppose that all individuals with $w \leq w_0$ and $w_0 > \underline{w}$ also choose to supply zero labour, so there are $H(0) > 0$ individuals earning zero income. Piketty and Saez (2013) show that the optimal marginal tax rate on these non-working individuals is

$$\frac{T'(0)}{1 - T'(0)} = \frac{g_0 - 1}{\varepsilon_0}, \text{ with } g_0 = \frac{W'(0)}{\lambda}, \varepsilon_0 = -\frac{1 - T'(0)}{H(0)} \frac{dH(0)}{d(1 - T'(0))},$$

where g_0 is the marginal social welfare weight on the non-working individuals in terms of government revenue and ε_0 is the elasticity of the number of non-working individuals with respect to the net of tax price. The numerator, $g_0 - 1$, again captures the equity effect of an increase in the marginal tax rate at the bottom and reflects the difference between the social benefit of a marginal increase in the consumption of the non-working and the fiscal cost of such an increase financed by an increase in $T'(0)$. The denominator ε_0 is the efficiency effect and reflects the behavioural responses to this change. Given that the government wants to redistribute from high- to low-income individuals, the marginal social welfare weights will be decreasing in income, and since the average marginal social welfare weight is equal to one, the marginal tax rate on the non-working individuals will necessarily be positive. The higher the marginal tax rate at the bottom of the income distribution, the greater the social welfare weight of those not working.

---

[17] The former follows because, by perturbing b incrementally, the average social value in terms of government revenue of giving everyone with income above $\underline{y}$ is simply one. The latter follows from noting that there is no one with income above $\bar{y}$ when the income distribution is bounded.

A maximin social welfare function also yields a positive marginal tax rate at the bottom in a non-linear income system even without bunching, as shown by Boadway and Jacquet (2008). Under maximin, no weight is put on the welfare of those with income greater than the lowest-income earner, that is, $G(y) = 0$ for all $y > \underline{y}$, and the optimal income tax rule for $y > \underline{y}$ is

$$\frac{T'(y)}{1 - T'(y)} = \frac{1 - H(y)}{\epsilon y h(y)}.$$

This expression is similar to that in (19) except for the equity term. Since no weight is put on the welfare of those with income greater than $\underline{y}$, there is no loss in social utility on their account when the marginal tax rate applying at y is increased. The equity term reflects only the social value of the increase in government revenue for all individuals between y and $\bar{y}$ when the marginal tax rate on y increases. When the marginal tax rate $T'(y)$ increases, all those above y, of whom there are $1 - H(y)$, pay the same increment in lump-sum tax revenue. Consequently, the marginal tax rate at the bottom of the income distribution will be positive and given by $T'(\underline{y}) = 1/(1 + \epsilon \underline{y} H(\underline{y})) > 0$. This implies a 100% marginal tax rate when $\underline{y} = 0$ so the lowest-wage individuals never work, and less than 100% when $\underline{y} > 0$.[18] With other social welfare functions, it is generally not possible to obtain further analytical results on the marginal tax rate schedule beyond those at the very bottom and very top of the wage distribution, and researchers have relied on numerical simulations to say something about the shape of the optimal marginal tax rate schedules.

The advantage of formulating the optimal income tax structure in terms of the income distribution rather than the wage distribution is that most parameters of the marginal income tax structure can be empirically observed. In the denominator, the elasticity of taxable income ϵ can be estimated with different empirical approaches as surveyed by Saez et al. (2012) and discussed further later. In the numerator of (19), the cumulative distribution $H(y)$ can be directly observed, while the social weights $G(y)$ must be assumed. However, it must be kept in mind that the income distribution is endogenous. Changing the assumed utility function or tax parameters will change the resulting income distribution whereas the underlying wage distribution is assumed to be exogenous.

The perturbation approach can be used to determine the optimal marginal tax rates applying to a range of incomes at the top and bottom of the income

---

[18] Boadway and Jacquet (2008) also show that optimal marginal tax schedule will be monotonically decreasing if the wage distribution is Pareto, Weibull or lognormal and approaches zero as w goes to $\bar{w}$. (If the distribution is Pareto and untruncated, the marginal tax rate is constant.) Moreover, total tax liabilities will be increasing in w, and the average income tax rate $T(y)/y$, which is more important for judging redistribution, will be single-peaked.

distribution, that is, when the income tax is piecewise linear. To see the former, consider a constant marginal tax rate $T'(y_T)$ that applies to incomes above y_T. The average income of those earning in this top income bracket will be given by $\bar{y}_T = \int_{y_T}^{\bar{y}} yh(y)dy/(1 - H(y_T))$. Consider a small increase $dT'(y_T) > 0$ at the optimum. This will not affect those earning incomes both below y_T and will increase the revenue raised from those with income above y_T by

$$dR = \left(\int_{y_T}^{\bar{y}} (y - y_T)h(y)dy \right) dT'(y_T).$$ This is the direct mechanical effect. The

total welfare cost of collecting this additional revenue is

$$dW = -g_T \left(\int_{y_T}^{\bar{y}} (y - y_T)h(y)dy \right) dT'(y_T),$$ where g_T is the average social welfare

weight of those earning more than y_T (weighted by income). Finally, the marginal increase in $T'(y_T)$ will reduce the earnings of those in the top income bracket, and the subsequent revenue cost of this behavioural effect is given by

$$dB = \left(1 - H(y_T) \right) T'(y_T)d\bar{y}_T,$$ where $d\bar{y}_T = \epsilon_T \bar{y}_T dT'(y_Y)/\left(1 - T'(y_T) \right)$ and

ϵ_T is the average elasticity (weighted by income) of those earning more than y_T with respect to the net of tax price, $1 - T'(y_T)$. Since this tax change is being considered at the optimum, it must be that $dR + dW + dB = 0$, which yields

$$\frac{T'(y_T)}{1 - T'(y_T)} = \frac{(1 - g_T)(\bar{y}_T - y_T)}{\epsilon_T \bar{y}_T}. \tag{20}$$

If the welfare weight on top income earners were zero ($g_T = 0$), (20) yields the tax revenue–maximizing rate. Its magnitude depends inversely on both the average elasticity of taxable of those in the top income bracket and on the expression $\bar{y}_T/(\bar{y}_T - y_T)$, which is the Pareto parameter (Saez, 2001).

Similarly, we can characterize the optimal marginal income tax rate applying over a range of income at the bottom of the income distribution. Assume a constant marginal tax rate $T'(y_B)$ applies to incomes below y_B. Let the average income of those in this bottom-income bracket be $\bar{y}_B = \int_{\underline{y}}^{y_B} yh(y)dy/H(y_B)$.

Now consider a small increase $dT'(y_B) > 0$ at the optimum. The marginal tax increase will affect those earning incomes both above and below y_B. The direct mechanical effect on revenue will be $dR =$

$$\left(\int_{\underline{y}}^{y_B} yh(y)dy + \left(1 - H(y_B) \right) \right) dT'(y_B).$$ The first term reflects the additional

revenue raised on those earning less than y_B. The second term reflects the fact that the marginal tax rates of those above y_B are held constant, but they pay an additional $dT'(y_B)$ in taxes on their inframarginal income. The total welfare cost of collecting this additional revenue is $dW = -g_B\left(\int_{\underline{y}}^{y_B} yh(y)dy\right)$ $dT'(y_B) - G(y_B)\left(1 - H(y_B)\right)dT'(y_B)$, where g_B is the average social welfare weight of those earning less than y_B (weighted by income). Assuming no income effects, the marginal increase in $T'(y_B)$ does not affect the income earned above y_B but reduces it for those earning less than y_B, and the subsequent revenue cost of this behavioural effect is given by $dB = H(y_B)T'(y_B)d\bar{y}_B$, where $d\bar{y}_B = \epsilon_B\bar{y}_BT'(y_B)/\left(1 - T'(y_B)\right)$ and ϵ_B is the average elasticity (weighted by income) of those earning less than y_B with respect to the net of tax price, $1 - T'(y_B)$. Given that this tax change is being considered at the optimum, it must be that $dR + dW + dB = 0$, which yields

$$\frac{T'(y_B)}{1 - T'(y_B)} = \frac{(1 - g_B)\bar{y}_BH(y_B) + \left(1 - G(y_B)\right)\left(1 - H(y_B)\right)}{\epsilon_B\bar{y}_BH(y_B)}. \tag{21}$$

The optimal tax rate applying to incomes below a certain threshold takes into account both the equity and efficiency effects in this bottom-income bracket in the standard way as given by the first term in the numerator and the denominator of (21), respectively. The optimal tax also reflects equity concerns for those earning more than the threshold as given by the second term in the numerator of (21). Since marginal tax rates are held constant for those earning income above y_B, there are no efficiency concerns arising from their behavioural responses. Rather, they all face a higher total tax liability since the marginal tax rate on income up to y_B is slightly higher. The fewer individuals earning more than y_B, the less revenue the government will raise from them, and the greater their social weight, the more concerned the government is about raising this additional tax revenue from them. In both cases, the optimal marginal tax rate in the bottom-income bracket will be positive but lower. If all individuals earned more than y_B, so $H(y_B) = 1$, then (21) reduces to the optimal linear progressive income tax rule given by (15).

Apps et al. (2014) demonstrate numerically that under a utilitarian social welfare function, the optimal two-bracket piecewise linear income tax system can result in either a convex (increasing marginal tax rates) or a non-convex (decreasing marginal tax rates) tax structure depending on the wage distribution and the elasticity of labour supply. With a Pareto wage distribution and a constant and identical elasticity of labour supply, marginal tax rates are higher in the top bracket than in the lower one. However, when the elasticity of labour supply is lower in the bottom eight wage deciles than in the top two, the marginal tax rate is higher in the lower tax bracket, which is intuitive. In contrast, when the wage distribution increases steeply at low wage rates and then follows the Pareto distribution at higher wages, the first-bracket marginal tax rate is now higher than the second-bracket rate. Numerical simulations in Bastani et al. (2019) show that under a maximin objective, marginal tax rates increase with income in a four-bracket piecewise linear tax system, while they decrease when the government maximizes the sum of the logs of individual utilities. In contrast, Slemrod et al. (1994) find that in the two-bracket case, the optimal marginal tax rate is higher at the bottom than at the top under both a utilitarian social welfare and a social welfare function with a finite inequality aversion.

3.2.6 Commodity Taxation: The Atkinson–Stiglitz Theorem

For simplicity, we follow Edwards et al. (1994) and Nava et al. (1996) and derive the Atkinson–Stiglitz theorem for a simple two-good, two-type case. Suppose there are two goods and leisure, so utility is $u(x_1, x_2, \ell)$, where ℓ denotes hours of work. Rewrite this in terms of goods and income for a person with wage w^i: $\mu^i(x_1, x_2, y) \equiv u(x_1, x_2, y/w^i)$. Assume there are two wage types of size n^1 and n^2 such that $w^2 > w^1$. Assume there is a non-linear income tax on y and a linear commodity tax on x_2 at the rate $\tau \gtreqless 0$. (Note that a tax on x_1 is redundant.) Define aggregate consumption, or disposable income, as $c \equiv y - T(y) = x_1 + (1 + \tau)x_2 = x_1 + q_2 x_2$, where producer prices are unity and $q_2 = 1 + \tau$.

A type$-i$ individual maximizes $\mu^i(x_1, x_2, y)$ subject to $x_1 + q_2 x_2 = c = y - T(y)$. Disaggregate the individual's problem into two stages. In the first stage, the individual chooses $y = w^i \ell$ and c, or equivalently labour supply since $c = y - T(y)$. In the second stage, c is allocated to x_1 and x_2. Solve these two stages in reverse order.

In the second stage, a type$-i$ individual takes c^i and y^i as given and chooses x_2 to maximize $\mu^i(c^i - q_2 x_2, x_2, y^i)$. The solution is a demand function $x_2^i = x_2(q_2, c^i, y^i)$, with $\partial x_2^i / \partial y^i \gtreqless 0$. The indirect utility function is $\nu^i(q_2, c^i, y^i)$ with $\nu_q^i = -x_2^i \mu_{x_1}^i$, $\nu_c^i = \mu_{x_1}^i$, $\nu_y^i = \mu_y^i$. We must allow for the possibility that a high-wage person will prefer to behave like a low-wage person if the income tax system redistributes enough. Denote the utility of a type-2 person who earns the income of a type-1 person as $\hat{\mu}^2(c^1 - q_2 \hat{x}_2, \hat{x}_2, y^1)$. The mimicker chooses $\hat{x}_2^2$ to maximize $\hat{\mu}^2(\cdot)$, which yields the demand function $\hat{x}_2^2(q_2, c^1, y^1)$

and the indirect utility function $\hat{v}^2(q_2, c^1, y^1)$. Note the important property that $\hat{x}_2^2 > x_2^1$ if x_2 is more complementary with leisure than x_1, and vice versa.

Turn now to the first stage. In practice, type$-i$ individuals anticipate the second stage and choose c^i and y^i to maximize $v^i(q_2, c^i, y^i)$ subject to $c^i = y^i - T(y^i)$. As above, we solve this directly by letting the government choose quantities c^1, y^1, c^2, y^2, and τ to maximize social welfare subject to budget and incentive compatibility constraints. Given the bundles the government offers, type$-i$ individuals choose their most preferred bundle (c^i, y^i). To solve this in the most instructive way, we disaggregate the government problem into two stages. First, it chooses the bundles c^1, y^1, c^2, and y^2, and therefore the optimal non-linear income tax, given τ. Then, we consider the welfare effect of changing τ, given that an optimal income tax is in place.

In the first stage, the government chooses c^1, y^1, c^2, and y^2, to maximize a social welfare function of form (9) subject to budget constraint and an incentive constraint $v^2(q_2, c^2, y^2) \geq \hat{v}^2(q_2, c^1, y^1)$ (which is the analogue of (17) in this case). The optimal income tax that solves this problem yields marginal effective tax rates on the two wage types that include two components: the marginal income tax rate and the marginal change in indirect tax revenues when incomes increase. The combined effective marginal tax rate has similar properties to marginal tax rates as in the standard case (e.g., a zero effective marginal tax rate at the top). Let the value function for the government's optimal income tax problem be $\Omega(\tau)$.

By the envelope function, $\partial\Omega(\tau)/\partial\tau = \partial\mathcal{L}/\partial\tau$, where $\mathcal{L}$ is the Lagrangian expression for the optimal income tax problem. Using the first-order conditions for the latter, we can derive

$$\frac{\partial\Omega(\tau)}{\partial\tau} = \gamma\hat{\mu}_{x_1}^2(\cdot)\left(\hat{x}_2^2 - x_2^1\right) + \lambda\tau\left(n^1\frac{\partial\tilde{x}_2^1}{\partial q_2} + n^2\frac{\partial\tilde{x}_2^2}{\partial q_2}\right),$$

where $\tilde{x}_j^i$ is the compensated for demand for x_j^i. Evaluating this at $\tau = 0$, we obtain

$$\frac{\partial\Omega(\tau)}{\partial\tau}\bigg|_{\tau=0} > 0 \text{ if } \hat{x}_2 > x_1.$$

From this, we obtain that $\tau > 0$ if x_2 is more complementary with leisure than is x_1. This is an analogue to the Corlett–Hague theorem and indicates the importance of the complementary/substitutability relationship between goods and leisure for determining the optimal tax structure. Suppose the utility function takes the weakly separable form $u(f(x_1, x_2), \ell)$. Then, $\hat{x}_2 = x_1$ since a type-2 mimicker differs from type−1 individual only in labour supplied, and therefore, $\tau = 0$. This result generalizes to more than two goods and two wage types and yields the *Atkinson–Stiglitz (1976) theorem:* optimal commodity taxes are uniform if preferences are weakly separable in labour. If we interpret consumption in different time periods to be different consumption goods, the Atkinson–Stiglitz theorem also implies that optimal capital income taxes should be zero.

Laroque (2005) and Kaplow (2006) generalized the Atkinson–Stiglitz theorem to instances where the existing income tax is not optimal. Suppose preferences are weakly separable in labour and goods and start with a differentiated commodity tax system and an arbitrary non-linear income tax. They show that a Pareto-improving tax reform can be achieved by making commodity taxes uniform and adjusting the income tax system appropriately. The result is the analogue of Hellwig (2010) for the case of a linear progressive income tax discussed above.

3.3 Extensive-Margin Labour Supply Approach

In the Mirrlees model, individuals are free to vary their labour supply in response to after-tax wage and income changes. In practice, workers may have limited discretion over hours of work. These restrictions have been captured in a stark way in extensive models of labour supply that limit individuals to discrete choices such as what kind of job to choose or whether to work at all. Diamond (1980) captured this in the most extreme way by assuming that individuals could only choose whether to participate in the labour market or not, and Saez (2002) explored to full consequences of this for the optimal tax structure. Saez, along with Rothschild and Scheuer (2013) and Ales et al. (2015), allowed individuals to choose not only whether to participate but also what job to take. In models of extensive-margin labour choice, there is a discrete number of job types. Income in each job is fixed and known to the government, for example, by taxpayer self-reporting. Disutility in each job if working or utility if unemployed can differ among individuals and is not observed by the government. As in the intensive-margin case, demand for workers is perfectly elastic, so anyone who chooses a job is guaranteed to get it at the given income.

3.3.1 Participation Choice Only

Begin with the simple case introduced by Diamond (1980) in which an individual's only choice is whether to participate in the labour force or be voluntarily unemployed. For each individual, there is only one job suited to their skills. Government tax-transfer policy consists of a tax contingent on each individual's income. Our analysis follows the assumptions adopted by Saez (2002).

Suppose there are n_i individuals of types $i = 0, \ldots, I$. The population is normalized to unity, so $\sum_{i \geq 0} n_i = 1$. An individual of type $i > 0$ can take a type–i job, which pays y_i and incurs a tax of $T_i \geq 0$, or can choose not to work, earn no income and obtain a transfer $-T_0$, which is option 0. Type–0 individuals are unable to work so necessarily choose option 0. Utility of work participants equals consumption, which for a type–i, worker is $c_i = y_i - T_i$. Utility if voluntarily unemployed is $c_0 + \widetilde{\delta}_i = -T_0 + \widetilde{\delta}_i$, where the value of leisure $\widetilde{\delta}_i \in [\underline{\delta}, \overline{\delta}]$ is distributed by $\Gamma_i(\delta_i)$. Thus, individuals differ by their utility of leisure that is unobservable to the government.

The marginal type–i participant is indifferent between participating or not, which implies that $y_i - T_i = -T_0 + \hat{\delta}$. All those with $\delta_i < \hat{\delta}_i$ choose to work. Therefore, the number of type–i participants is $n_i \Gamma_i(\hat{\delta}_i) = n_i \Gamma_i(y_i - T_i + T_0) \equiv h_i(\cdot)$, and the number of non-participants is $1 - \sum_{i \geq 0} n_i \Gamma_i(y_i - T_i + T_0) \equiv h_0$. Note that participation is a function of $y_i - T_i + T_0 = c_i - c_0$, that is, the gain in consumption from participating.

We assume that for social welfare purposes, the government gives full weight to the utility that non-participants obtain from leisure, which varies among individuals. This is not an innocuous assumption since it assumes that those who get more benefit from leisure obtain correspondingly more weight in the social welfare function. Social utility for participants is $W(c_i) = W(y_i - T_i)$, and that for non-participants is $W(c_0 + \widetilde{\delta}_i) = W(-T_0 + \widetilde{\delta}_i)$. Social welfare analogous to (9), is

$$\mathcal{W}(\cdot) = \sum_{i \geq 1} h_i(y_i - T_i + T_0) W(y_i - T_i) + \sum_{i \geq 0} h_i \int_{\hat{\delta}_i}^{\overline{\delta}} W(-T_0 + \delta_i) d\Gamma_i(\delta_i)$$

where the first term includes the participants and the second term the non-participants.

The government chooses taxes and transfers $T_0, \ldots, T_i, \ldots, T_I$ to maximize social welfare subject to its budget constraint:

$$\sum_{i \geq 1} h_i(y_i - T_i + T_0) T_i + \left(1 - \sum_{i \geq 1} h_i(y_i - T_i + T_0)\right) T_0 = R.$$

Define *marginal social weights in terms of government revenue* for participants and non-participants, respectively, as follows:[19]

---
[19] Note that g_i is equivalent to $\alpha(w)/\lambda$ where $\alpha(w)$ is defined in (13).

$$g_i \equiv \frac{W_i'}{\lambda} \text{ and } g_0 \equiv \frac{1}{h_0}\left(\frac{W_0'}{\lambda} + \sum_{i \geq 1} n_i \int_{\hat{\delta}_i}^{\bar{\delta}} \frac{W_{i0}'}{\lambda} d\Gamma_i\right),$$

where λ is the Lagrange multiplier on the government budget constraint. The marginal social welfare weight for non-participants is the average marginal social welfare weight in terms of government revenue across all those not working, including both the type-0 s who are unable to work and those type$-i$ individuals, $i \geq 1$, who choose not to work. Define the *elasticity of participation* for a type$-i$ individual as

$$\eta_i \equiv \frac{(y_i - T_i + T_0)h_i'(y_i - T_i + T_0)}{h_i(y_i - T_i + T_0)} = \frac{(c_i - c_0)}{h_i(c_i - c_0)}\frac{dh_i(c_i - c_0)}{d(c_i - c_0)}.$$

This is the proportionate change in the number of participants $h_i(\cdot)$ from a proportionate change in the consumption gain from participation, $c_i - c_0$. The size of η_i depends on the distribution of the utility of leisure δ_i of which little is known.

Using these definitions, the first-order conditions for the choice of T_i reduce to

$$\frac{T_i - T_0}{c_i - c_0} \equiv \frac{\tau(y_i)}{1 - \tau(y_i)} = \frac{1 - g_i}{\eta_i} = \frac{\text{equity}}{\text{efficiency}}, \quad i \geq 1, \tag{22}$$

$$\sum_{i \geq 0} h_i g_i = 1, \tag{23}$$

where $\tau(y_i) = (T_i - T_0)/y_i$ is the *participation tax rate* at income level y_i, that is, the increase in tax liability when changing from non-participation to participation. Equations (22) and (23) have the following implications. Suppose that non-participants have the highest social weight, say, because it includes those unable to work, so $g_0 > g_1 > \ldots > g_I$. Then, since the average value of the g_is is unity by (23), there is some i^* such that $g_{i^*} = 1$. For all, $i < i^*$, $g_i > 1$, so from (22), $T_i < T_0 < 0$. That is, the participation tax rate is negative. The transfer of $-T_0$ to the type-0s is smaller than the income transfers to the working poor, $-T_i$ for $i < i^*$. This has been used to rationalize participation subsidies such as the Earned Income Tax Credit in the USA, the Working Tax Credit in the United Kingdom and the Canada Worker Benefit.

It is possible, however, that the social weight put on non-participants is high enough that $g_0 > 1$ and $g_i \leq 1$ for all $i \geq 1$ so the participation tax is everywhere non-negative. This is the case if the social welfare function is maximin, and the type-0s are the least well-off. In these cases, $g_i = 0$ for all $i > 0$, so $T_i > T_0$ for all i. Thus, for a participation subsidy to be optimal, the social welfare weight must be higher for non-participants than participants, but not high enough that $g_i < 1$ for all participants.

If, for example, a high proportion of non-participants have higher skills, it is possible that g_0 is lower than g_i for low-income participants. Christiansen (2015) shows, using a utilitarian social welfare function, that the optimality of a larger transfer to the working poor than to the non-working hinges crucially on a sufficiently high participation elasticity of those individuals with productivity just above the productivity of the working poor. By reducing the transfer to the non-working relative to the working poor, the government increases the incentive of those with slightly higher productivity than the non-working poor to participate in the labour market. The more responsive the participation of these individuals, the greater the potential gain from having them working. At the opposite extreme, if all individuals with productivity greater than type-1 always worked, then g_1 would necessarily be less than one.

These results are based on the assumption that individuals differ in their preferences for leisure. Choné and Laroque (2005) assume instead that individuals differ in their *taste for work*, which is modelled as the financial compensation needed to work. All unemployed individuals are equally well-off, and since individuals choose whether to work or not, those who are voluntarily unemployed are the worst-off. A government with a maximin objective, as Choné and Laroque assume, therefore maximizes the welfare of the voluntarily unemployed. In this case, a participation subsidy at the bottom is generally not desirable. That lack of support for a participation subsidy applies to the utilitarian case as well, where the utility of participants now counts in social welfare. Lack of empirical evidence about whether individuals differ in their preferences for work or for leisure, and how such preferences vary with individual productivity weakens the case for negative participation taxes at low-income levels.

3.3.2 Participation and Occupational Choice

The case for participation subsidies is weakened further when we allow individuals to choose more than participation. Suppose they can decide both whether to participate in the job market and in which occupation. Saez (2002) assumes individuals of a given skill can choose an occupation of the next lower skill. Thus, type$-i$ individuals who participate can choose job i or job $i - 1$. Labour supplied to occupation i can be depicted by the function $h_i(c_i - c_0, c_{i+1} - c_i, c_i - c_{i-1})$. The first argument captures the participation margin, while the latter two capture occupational choice margins. The partial elasticity of $h_i(\cdot)$ with respect to $c_i - c_0$ is η_i as before, and the elasticity with respect to $c_i - c_{i-1}$ is denoted ζ_i. Using a similar approach to the previous one, optimal taxes satisfy

$$\frac{T_i - T_{i-1}}{c_i - c_{i-1}} = \frac{1}{\zeta_i h_i} \sum_{j=1}^{I} h_j \left[1 - g_j - \eta_j \frac{T_j - T_0}{c_j - c_0} \right], \quad i \geq 1, \tag{24}$$

where the left-hand side is the tax rate arising from the job choice decision and the tax term on the right-hand side is the participation tax as above. In this case, a participation subsidy for type-1 individuals is optimal only if the participation elasticities η_i are large enough relative to the job choice elasticity ζ_1.

To gain insight into whether a participation subsidy is optimal, evaluate (24) at $i = 1$ and use the normalization of the welfare weights $\sum_{j=0}^{I} g_j h_j = 1$ to obtain

$$\frac{T_1 - T_0}{c_1 - c_0} = \frac{1}{h_1(\zeta_1 + \eta_1)} \left[(g_0 - 1)h_0 - \sum_{j=1}^{I} h_j \eta_j \frac{T_j - T_0}{c_j - c_0} \right]. \tag{25}$$

Equation (25) generalizes the insight from the pure extensive-margin model of Christiansen (2015) that the optimality of a negative participation tax at the bottom depends critically on the participation elasticities of those workers with productivity above that of the working poor (types $j > 1$).

Alternatively, suppose, following Jacquet et al. (2013) and Choné and Laroque (2011), that individuals choose both whether to participate in a job suitable to their skill and how intensively to work. Not surprisingly, Jacquet et al. find that combining an extensive decision with the standard intensive model reduces marginal income tax rates, resulting in less progressivity, and reduces the possibility that a participation subsidy is optimal. Choné and Laroque show that work subsidies for low-skilled individuals can be optimal provided the social welfare weights on workers decrease both in incomes and productivity. This relies on several assumptions on the underlying distribution of work opportunities, including being log-concave, for which there is a lack of empirical support.

To summarize, when individuals choose both whether to participate and how much labour to supply, the case for a participation subsidy at the bottom is weaker, and the income tax is less progressive than when only participation is chosen. This is in addition to the case for participation subsidy being eliminated if non-participants have a lower social weight than participants or if non-participants have a very high social weight as in the maximin case. A further caveat to the case for participation subsidies arises when participation does not guarantee that a job will be landed. We return to this later.

Finally, having labour supply decisions on the extensive margin does not affect the policy implications for commodity taxation: both the Deaton result for linear income taxes and the Atkinson–Stiglitz theorem for non-linear taxes generalize to the extensive-margin case.

4 Extensions to the Optimal Income Tax Approach

There have been many applications of optimal tax analysis. Pigouvian tax rules can be obtained by allowing the consumption or production of some goods to emit externalities. Optimal rules for the provision of public goods can be derived by making government expenditures endogenous. Optimal tax rules will then incorporate the marginal costs of public funds. Specifying the production side of the economy by introducing firms leads to optimal business taxation. Making the economy dynamic and uncertain leads to the possibility of taxing capital income and risk, as well as wealth and wealth transfer taxation. We do not have the space to deal adequately with these or other extensions. Instead, we briefly consider four extensions of the standard optimal tax analysis. In each case, we emphasize intuition and policy relevance rather than technical analysis.

4.1 Intertemporal Optimal Taxation

Consider a simple two-period setting in which an individual chooses labour income and consumes some of it in the first period and saves and consumes the rest in the second period. This is equivalent to a setting with two goods (one in each period) and first-period leisure (or labour), where the price of leisure is the wage rate and the price of second-period consumption is $1/(1+r)$. A tax on capital income is like a tax on second-period consumption. As mentioned previously, the Atkinson–Stiglitz theorem implies that if preferences are weakly separable in goods and leisure, first- and second-period consumption should be taxed at the same rate. A positive capital income tax would be optimal if second-period consumption and first-period leisure are complements.

Once we adopt different assumptions, there is a case for a tax on capital income even if preferences are weakly separable, as Banks and Diamond (2010) show. A tax on capital income will be optimal if higher-skilled taxpayers have lower utility discount rates, so have higher propensities to save. If individuals earn income in more than one period and if future wages are uncertain and cannot be insured, capital income taxation is optimal. A reduction in savings makes it more difficult for high-wage workers to mimic low-wage workers in the second period. Taxing capital income is also desirable in multiperiod models where individuals face credit constraints that prevents them from borrowing to finance future consumption. A higher capital income tax in the second period entails lower-wage taxation in the first, so the liquidity constraint is relaxed. Capital income taxation is optimal if individuals obtain bequests that are not taxed. Finally, capital income taxation would also be optimal if rates of return on an individual's savings increased with the amount of their savings or with their skills (e.g., entrepreneurial skills). In all these cases, there is no presumption that the optimal capital income tax rate is as high as the optimal earnings tax rate.

Recently, many economists have advocated a wealth tax as a way to address large inequalities of wealth. Scheuer and Slemrod (2021) summarize the arguments. As they point out, a wealth tax is equivalent to a capital income tax if all taxpayers have the same rate of return on savings. If A is asset wealth, a wealth tax of t_w will yield revenues of $t_w A$, while a capital income tax t_k will yield $t_k r A$. Therefore, a capital tax t_k is equivalent to a wealth tax $t_w = t_k r$. If r is the same for all taxpayers, there is nothing to be gained by using a wealth tax instead of a capital income tax.

However, if r differs among taxpayers, a wealth tax will impose a lower tax rate on the capital income of those with a higher r compared with a capital income tax, and vice versa. If a higher r reflects greater productivity, a wealth tax will favour high-productivity investors and will result in a substitution of high-income investments for low-income ones. Guvenen et al. (2019) show using a calibrated model for the USA that a wealth tax may dominate a capital income tax in these circumstances. On the other hand, if differences in r across taxpayers reflect rents or unexpected returns, a capital income tax will dominate a wealth tax because it will capture more of the rents.

4.2 Interdependent Utility Functions

Utility functions are interdependent when the outcomes of one person directly affect the utility of another (rather than through prices). This can reflect altruism, envy, paternalism or simply having preferences over another person's choices. Choices resulting from interdependent utility functions may be observable, as with bequests, charitable donations, dependent care or voluntary work. Interdependent utility can also influence the purchase of positional or status goods and the supply of labour to keep up with one's neighbours. Decision-making within families is especially influenced by interdependent utility. However, some forms of interdependent utility are not revealed by individual behaviour, including admiration or envy of one's neighbours or a distaste of their choices. Preferences over social outcomes are also not directly observable except through polling or voting choices.

The policy problem is how to treat utility interdependence. The issues are complex and controversial. Nonetheless, it is worth noting some of them even if we cannot be categorical about tax policy prescriptions. Some argue that all decisions reflect the revealed preferences of individuals, so should be included as individual utility for social welfare purposes (Kaplow, 2008). Others argue that decisions made to fulfill interdependent utility preferences should not be included in the decision-maker's social welfare function because that gives rise to double-counting (Hammond, 1987; Milgrom, 1993). Thus, voluntary transfers would count as utility to both donors and recipients.

Our view, discussed in Boadway and Cuff (2015), is that counting the benefits of both donors and recipients in social welfare is questionable. Although the revealed-preference argument for double-counting is on the surface persuasive, there are compelling arguments against it. The benefit to a donor from the utility gains of a recipient should then apply to any form of interdependent utility whether revealed through transfers or not. Family members value the well-being of each other, but there is no suggestion that this multiplicity of utilities be counted in social welfare. The same applies to feelings of altruism or envy toward fellow citizens. Mirrlees (2007) notes the analogy between saving for one's own future and saving for heirs. He argues that we would not consider counting the utility we obtain now when saving for our future self. Some might regard the role of government redistribution as reflecting the altruism of the rich for the poor and internalizing the free-riding from private donations (Hochman and Rodgers, 1969). There is no suggestion that in this case, the rich taxpayers' altruism should be counted as social welfare in addition to the benefits of the transfer recipients. Voluntary transfers may not give utility to donors at all. They may represent voluntary transfers done out of a sense of obligation, making the donors worse off.

Decisions taken for interdependent utility motives can have policy consequences. For example, voluntary transfers such as bequests or charitable donations affect both equity and efficiency. From an equity perspective, such transfers represent income to recipients that can be used for consumption and other purposes. For the donors, if the transfers are considered to represent utility benefits, they should be treated as consumption. However, if donors are regarded as forgoing utility when they make transfers, these should be deducted from their income. Efficiency consequences arise if one regards the transfers as yielding utility to the donors. If so, voluntary transfers simultaneously benefit the donors and the recipients, but the donors only take into account their own benefit. This constitutes an efficient case for subsidizing voluntary transfers (Diamond, 2006; Kaplow, 2008). In practice, charitable donations are typically subsidized, while bequests are not, which is inconsistent. Potentially, the social welfare consequences of intra-family transfers are large. A transfer from one family member to another provides altruistic benefits to all family members so is like a public good. In principle, all such benefits of family transfers would have to be taken into account, which is potentially contentious, and in any case infeasible since most such transfers cannot be observed by the government.

Similar conceptual issues arise with the consumption of status or positional goods and with "rat-race" labour supply. Most studies assume that the personal benefit from consuming status goods or from keeping up with the income of one's neighbour should not count as social welfare. Layard (1980) notes that if utility depends on status and income reflects status, income taxation is justified on both equity and efficiency grounds. It reduces excessive work due to status-seeking and increases social welfare. Frank (2005) discusses the negative consequences of utility depending on relative consumption. Consumers spend too much on "positional goods" (goods that signal consumers' position in a status ranking), which only changes their status ranking, rather than increasing their material well-being. Increasing taxation of these goods can be difficult, but increasing income tax progressivity reduces spending on luxury positional goods relative to more material goods while leaving individuals in the same relative position as before. On the other hand, if status goods were to be included in social welfare, the tax system should be less progressive.

Some authors study the implications of interdependent utility for optimal income taxation. Oswald (1983) analyzes the Mirrlees optimal tax problem when individual utility functions include a term for either altruism or jealousy, and these terms count as social welfare. Marginal tax rates increase with jealousy and decline with altruism and can be negative in the latter case. Nishimura (2003) assumes that in addition to maximizing social welfare, the planner wants to restrict envy in the sense of individuals preferring others' consumption bundles. He adds limited envy as a constraint, which is binding for optimal income tax allocations in which high-income individuals are better off. This results in higher marginal income tax rates as well as higher commodity tax rates on goods preferred by low-wage individuals, which reduces the envy of the high-wage types. Kanbur and Tuomala (2013) consider the case where individuals' well-being depends on their income relative to the average. Using theory and simulations, they show that as individuals put more weight on relative income, the progressivity of optimal marginal income taxation also increases, that is, marginal tax rates rise faster with income and the average tax rate at the bottom becomes more negative. They also find that this increase in marginal tax rates due to relativity is dampened as pre-tax inequality increases.

4.3 Different Preferences

A vexing issue in optimal tax analysis is how to deal with differences in preferences. For example, suppose individuals put differing preference weights on leisure. Individuals with the same wage rate earn different incomes depending on their preferences for leisure, and high-wage persons with high preferences for leisure may earn the same income as low-wage persons with low preferences for leisure. Optimal redistribution will differ depending on the social weight put on preferences for leisure.

One approach to differences in preferences is to neither reward nor punish individuals based on their preferences. The policy should aim to redistribute among individuals to compensate only for differences in characteristics over which they have no control, such as wage rates or skills – the *principle of compensation*. At the same time, they should neither be rewarded nor penalized for characteristics over which they have control – the *principle of responsibility*. Individuals are typically assumed to have control over their preferences (Fleurbaey and Maniquet, 2011), though with some limits resulting from their socio-economic backgrounds (Roemer, 1998). Despite the attractiveness of these two principles, they cannot generally both be satisfied at the same time. For example, suppose there are two wage types (high- and low-wage) and two preference types (high and low taste for leisure), and assume the government can observe each individual's wage-preference type. For each preference type, utilities should be equalized by lump-sum transfers (the principle of compensation); for each wage type, individuals of different preferences should get the same transfer (the principle of responsibility). It is straightforward to show geometrically that these two policies cannot be satisfied at the same time (Boadway, 2012, p. 214).

Fleurbaey and Maniquet (2011) take the approach that while the two principles cannot both be satisfied, one could be fully satisfied and the other partially. Suppose the principle of compensation is satisfied fully, and the principle of responsibility only partially. Full compensation is achieved by an equal-preferences transfer. Imagine two individuals with the same preferences and different wage rates supplying the same labour but obtaining different consumption. An equal-preferences transfer that reduces their consumption differences while holding the labour supply constant improves social welfare. Fleurbaey and Maniquet capture partial responsibility by laissez-faire selection, which says that if all individuals had the same skills but different preferences, laissez-faire would be socially optimal. The social welfare ordering must also satisfy the Pareto principle and the independence of irrelevant alternatives. Fleurbaey and Maniquet show that these imply a maximin social ordering with the least well-off individuals being those with the lowest wage rate and the weakest preferences for leisure. Different characterizations of partial responsibility result in the individual with the lowest wage and the highest preference for leisure being considered the worst-off.

Fleurbaey and Maniquet also consider cases where responsibility is full and compensation partial. Their approach emphasizes the need to establish a set of principles that determine who is the least well-off and therefore most deserving of transfers. As a methodology for addressing differences in preferences, it is useful, but it provides limited guidance from a policy perspective. While the least well-off persons include those with the lowest wage rate, whether the most deserving are those with the lowest or highest preference for leisure depends on the assumptions adopted.

In designing the tax system to deal with differences in preferences, two difficult problems arise. First, preferences are not directly observable, though they affect behaviour. At best, the government may elicit such information at a cost by monitoring (Boadway and Cuff, 1999) or by separating contracts (Blackorby and Donaldson, 1988). In the optimal income tax literature, the government cannot identify persons with different preferences but can condition the tax system on knowledge it has about the distribution of preferences.

Second, aggregating individuals with different preferences into a social welfare function is conceptually problematic. The pattern of optimal marginal tax rates can vary significantly according to the weight put on different preference groups (Boadway et al., 2000b; Cuff, 2000; Choné and Laroque, 2010). If individuals with a low preference for leisure are given a high weight, the optimal tax system may redistribute from lower- to higher-income persons at the bottom end, resulting in negative marginal tax rates. The problem is compounded by the fact that some persons earning little or no income are unable to work due to disability but might nonetheless have a strong preference for working if they could.

4.4 Tagging

The standard optimal income tax literature assumes that individuals only differ in their wage rates. In practice, they can vary in other characteristics that are relevant for policy. In the simplest case, individuals can be divided into groups according to some identifiable indicator, or *tag*. The tag may be an imperfect indicator of some underlying characteristic of interest. In the original tagging literature due to Akerlof (1978), individuals differed in their ability to work. Some individuals may be unable to work or may only be able to work a limited amount due to disability or social conventions. The optimal transfer to the disabled relative to those who are able but choose not to work depends upon a value judgment. In practice, the disabled are typically eligible for a higher transfer than the voluntary unemployed, assuming they can be identified. The disabled require a higher income to attain the same level of utility as those voluntarily unemployed given that they face a higher cost of living.[20] As well, transfers to the voluntary employed may be held below the first-best optimal level in order to discourage able workers from choosing not to work. If the government can observe who is disabled, the incentive constraint that precludes the able from choosing not to work will not apply, and the disabled can be given a higher transfer. If the government cannot identify who is disabled, it must make the same transfer to those unable to work and the voluntary unemployed. This was the assumption in the extensive-margin optimal income tax approach discussed above.

One way to address this information issue is to assume that the government can acquire some information that enables the incentive constraint to be relaxed. Following Akerlof (1978) and Parsons (1996), assume that an observable signal or *tag* exists that is positively correlated with disability. Transfer recipients can be divided into tagged and untagged groups, with those tagged having a higher proportion of disabled relative to able persons. Within each group, transfers to those not working are limited by an incentive constraint, but lump-sum transfers can be made between groups. Under a utilitarian social objective, transfers are made from the untagged to the tagged group until the average marginal utility of income in each group is equal. However, inter-group redistribution creates inequality: the untagged disabled are made worse off (type-1 statistical errors), while the tagged able become better off (type-2 errors). If aversion to inequality increases, the transfer from the untagged to the tagged group falls, reducing the value of tagging. In the limit, with a maximin objective, tagging would be of no use since it makes some of the disadvantaged worse off.

The value of tagging is limited by other factors besides aversion to inequality. The less accurate is tagging – especially the more type-1 errors – the less valuable it is. Some may object to tagging on horizontal equity grounds since otherwise identical persons are treated differently depending on whether they are tagged, though for others social welfare overrules horizontal equity concerns (Kaplow, 2001). The value of tagging may be further compromised if a stigma attaches to being tagged (Jacquet and Van der Linden, 2006). The stigma may reflect the shame of being identified as tagged, even if only the

---

[20] However, Sen (1973) has pointed out that a utilitarian government may choose to transfer less to the disabled than to the able unemployed. It will seek to equalize the marginal utility of consumption among transfer recipients, and that may entail higher transfers to those who are most able to convert income into utility.

tagging administrator observes it. The stigma may also result from type-2 errors. Public knowledge that some non-deserving persons receive transfers may throw suspicion on all transfer recipients. The failure of needy persons to be tagged may reflect low application or take-up rates due to cost or complexity. Complexity may even be used to discourage non-deserving applicants from applying (Kleven and Kopczuk, 2011). Finally, agency problems between the government and tagging administrators may compromise the accuracy of tagging (Boadway et al., 1999).

The principle of tagging has been taken up in the optimal income taxation literature. Some observable characteristics may allow policy-makers to divide taxpayers into identifiable groups, each with different skill distributions. Characteristics include age (Banks and Diamond, 2010; Weinzierl, 2011), gender (Cremer et al., 2010), parental status (Bastani et al., 2019) and region of residence (Gordon and Cullen, 2012). The population is divided into two or more identifiable groups, and an optimal income tax applies within each group with intergroup redistribution. As long as the distribution of skills differs across groups, social welfare can be enhanced by tagging, possibly even if the social welfare function is maximin (Boadway and Pestieau, 2007). The properties of income taxes in each group vary with the specific application. Immonen et al. (1998), using simulation techniques, find that marginal tax rates increase with skills in the group with higher average skills but decline in the other group. Boadway and Pestieau (2007), using a two-type example, show that the income tax should be more progressive in the group with higher average skills. Cremer et al. (2010), who tag by gender, find in a model calibrated to US data that higher-skilled males would lose from tagging. Some may object to tagging by gender or other characteristics on grounds of discrimination. Banks and Diamond (2010) argue that this objection does not apply to age, since everyone experiences different ages over their lifetime.

5 Estimating the Optimal Income Tax Structure

The solution to the optimal income tax problem reflects the trade-off between efficiency and equity. The former depends on the behavioural response of taxpayers to income taxation, and the latter depends upon the social weights that the government places on income changes by income group. In this section, we review the methods used in the optimal income tax literature to estimate behavioural effects and determine social welfare weights.

5.1 Empirical Analysis of Behavioural Responses

The efficiency losses from redistribution depend on individuals' responses to taxation, which can be captured by behavioural elasticities. These elasticities can be estimated empirically. One approach, following the labour economics literature, focuses on estimating labour supply responses to taxes (see Keane (2011) for a survey of this literature).[21] There is also a growing public economics literature estimating the elasticity of taxable income and participation responses to transfer programs. We briefly review the latter literature.

5.1.1 Estimates of the Elasticity of Taxable Income

The optimal income tax rate formulas are typically derived from models in which taxable income is determined solely from labour supply decisions. In reality, individuals make decisions along many different margins that affect their taxable income, such as the timing of income receipt, the shifting of income between income sources that are taxed at differential rates, undertaking other forms of tax avoidance, or simply not declaring income. Rather than trying to determine the specific margin along which individuals change their taxable income, researchers instead focus on estimating how total taxable income responds to tax changes, which can be captured by the elasticity of taxable income.

Suppose preferences are defined over disposable income c and reported taxable income z and represented by the utility function $u(c,y)$. Saez et al. (2012) define a linearized budget constraint at the chosen point as $c = (1 - t) + E$, where t is the marginal tax rate and E is the individual's virtual income. The individual's maximization problem yields reported taxable income y as a function of the net-of-tax price $1 - t$ and virtual income E, and we define the *elasticity of taxable income* (ETI) as

$$\text{ETI} = \frac{\partial y}{\partial (1-t)} \frac{1-t}{y}.$$

The ETI captures all behavioural responses to changes in t and could reflect not just changes in labour supply but also tax avoidance or tax evasion behaviour. Without income effects, the ETI also provides a measure of the efficiency costs of income taxation. Feldstein (1999) has argued that as long as it is costly for an individual to evade or avoid taxes, the welfare cost of changes in income is the same as for changes in labour supply, as long as the individual is behaving

---

[21] Spadaro et al. (2015), Table 4, summarize the existing empirical estimates of the extensive (participation) and intensive labour supply elasticities for single individuals.

optimally. In that sense, the elasticity of taxable income is a *sufficient statistic* for measuring the efficiency costs of taxation: there is no need to disentangle the components of the change in income (Chetty, 2009). However, Chetty also argues that not all changes in income represent efficiency losses. Some are transfers in income to lower-income levels and thus only partly avoid taxes, while others represent postponement of tax liabilities. Still, others may result in penalty payments to the government. Thus, the observed ETI can overestimate the efficiency costs of tax changes.[22]

Saez et al. (2012) survey the empirical approaches used in estimating the ETI and summarize selective findings. They note that the literature typically ignores income effects on the grounds that there is no general agreement as to their size.[23] Using a share analysis, which examines the effect of a tax change on the share of income accruing to the top 1% of income earners while controlling for other factors, the US evidence suggests that the ETI of these top income earners is between 0.58 and 0.82. Saez and Veall (2005) find an estimate of around 0.47 using Canadian data from 1920 to 2000 but a much smaller elasticity when looking only at the share of the top 1% of wage income. Wage income is more subject to third-party reporting and has fewer tax avoidance opportunities relative to capital income. Estimates of the ETI have been used to inform policy debates about taxing the rich (Diamond and Saez, 2011; Veall, 2012). Much less focus has been on the bottom of the income distribution.

Focusing on lower-income earners in the USA, Saez (2010) uses a bunching analysis on the Earned Income Tax Credit (EITC), which is the largest transfer program to low-income families. The transfer increases with income, reaches a plateau and then is phased out. Its size also increases with the number of children in the family. Saez documents significant bunching of reported income around the income level where the EITC is first maximized. The estimated elasticities from this observed bunching depend on the number of children (0.21 for 1 child and 0.15 for 2 or more children) but are largely driven by self-employed income (1.1 and 0.8 for 1 and 2 or more children, respectively). Estimated elasticities for the self-employed increase over the period under study, but those for wage earners – who likely have little influence over their income and who are subject to third-party reporting – remain close to zero over the entire period. Saez et al. (2012) conclude that the ETI for the USA lies

---

[22] Even without income effects, the ETI may not be a sufficient statistic for the efficiency cost of income taxation if some behavioural responses result in either additional revenue or positive externalities. For example, there may be shifting of income to other tax bases or to future tax bases, the claiming of deductions that have positive social benefits such as charitable giving, or tax evasion may involve potential financial penalties (Chetty, 2009).

[23] Two exceptions are Gruber and Saez (2002) and Kleven and Schultz (2014) who estimate very small income effects for reported income using US and Danish panel tax data, respectively.

somewhere between 0.12 and 0.4. The midpoint of 0.25 is often used in calibrations with an assumed higher elasticity for top income earners (Gordon and Cullen, 2012).

5.1.2 Estimates of Participation Responses

Kleven (2019) studied the effect of EITC changes in the USA on participation rates among single women with varying numbers of children. He considered all federal and state changes to EITC since the program was introduced in 1975. Participation rates of single women with children showed a pronounced increase around 1993 and closed the gap with childless single women. Subsequently, participation rates for the two groups changed very little. This coincided with a significant increase in the maximum EITC credit, particularly for families with two or more children. To what extent was this increase in participation rates for single women with children due to 1993 EITC reforms? Kleven's empirical analysis takes into account other confounding factors, including major welfare reforms of the early 1990s and the buoyant economy. His result suggests that virtually all changes in participation can be attributed to these confounding factors, and none to EITC changes.

The absence of labour supply effects of EITC could be because of low participation elasticities or of lack of information about the program. Recipients are unlikely to know how they are affected by EITC when they consider labour market decisions because the program is complicated and is only effective over a limited range of low incomes. The provision of information on the EITC to potential EITC recipients by tax preparers was the focus of a field experiment by Chetty and Saez (2013). Their study was motivated by what was at the time a generally accepted finding of strong participation responses to the EITC but marginal or zero earning responses. The authors find virtually no effect from providing information on subsequent earnings of potential EITC recipients. They did, however, find evidence that the earning responses to the information provided depended on the tax professional, which suggests administrators of tax-transfer programs can have real effects on how individuals respond to these programs.

5.2 Inferring Social Welfare Functions

The structure of the optimal income tax system is sensitive to the assumed social welfare function. When considering tax policies for actual economies, the question is: How does society value the well-being of individuals with differing incomes? Two main approaches have been used to try to uncover the relevant objectives of government in practice. The first is the *optimal inverse approach* that determines the implied social welfare weights from the actual tax-transfer system chosen by the government. The underlying assumption is that the government uses a social welfare function in choosing actual tax policy. The second is the *stated-preference approach* that surveys individuals for their views on different social objectives. How one then aggregates these individual preferences into a social objective that could be used for tax policy evaluations remains an open question.

5.2.1 Optimal Inverse Approach

In this approach, social preferences that would generate the existing tax system are estimated given assumptions about individual preferences, production technology and skill distributions. This approach was first used in the context of optimal commodity taxation by Christiansen and Jansen (1978) using Norwegian data and extended to optimal income taxation by Bourguignon and Spadaro (2012) using French data.

To understand this approach, suppose the utility function is quasilinear in consumption with isoelastic labour supply as given by (18). The optimal tax rule (19) can then be solved for the marginal social welfare weight of all individuals with labour earnings greater than y as a function of the observed tax schedule and the income distribution (see Lockwood and Weinzierl 2016):

$$g(y) = \frac{W'(y)}{\lambda} = 1 + \frac{T'(y)}{1 - T'(y)} \epsilon \left(1 + \frac{yh'(y)}{h(y)} \right).$$

The last term is the elasticity of the density of the income distribution at income y, which can be determined empirically (Bastani and Lundberg, 2017). Using the actual tax system, observed income distribution and an estimated elasticity of taxable income, a marginal social welfare weight can be obtained at each income y.

The inversion approach can also be extended to the case where individuals make discrete participation and job choice decisions as discussed previously. The optimal tax rule is now given by (24) that involves elasticities of participation η_i and job choice ζ_i. The marginal social welfare weight for $i = I$ can be derived directly from (24) as a function of observed income levels, taxes and elasticities and is given by

$$g_I = 1 - \eta_I \frac{T_I - T_0}{c_I - c_0} - \zeta_I \frac{T_I - T_{I-1}}{c_I - c_{I-1}}.$$

With g_I in hand, one can solve recursively for the marginal social welfare weight for the $i = 1, \ldots, I - 1$ groups using (24). Finally, g_0 can be obtained given the normalization of the marginal social welfare weights in (23) (Bourguignon and Spadaro, 2012).

Two key issues that papers using this approach have studied are (a) whether marginal social welfare weights estimated from actual tax systems imply a social welfare function that is Paretian, that is, exhibits non-negative marginal social welfare weights, and (b) whether the government puts less weight on higher-income persons, that is, marginal social welfare weights decreasing in income.[24] The research to date shows that there is far from a single structure of social welfare weights implied by existing tax-benefit systems across all countries, but that they follow a general pattern with weights associated with the non-working being possibly the highest, and weights falling in the working poor or bottom-income earner groups and then remaining relatively constant or falling in income. The pattern varies across countries. The highest income groups have the lowest weights, but they may still be quite high and positive (as in the USA) or negative (as in Sweden).

5.2.2 Stated Preference Approach

A more direct way to solicit social preferences is to ask people for their redistribution preferences as is done in the General Social Survey in the USA, the European Social Survey in several European countries, and the World Values Survey in several other countries. These surveys ask individuals for their views about the role of government in redistributing income either to ensure everyone (or just the poor) is provided for or to reduce income inequality. Individuals are asked to respond along a numerical scale that corresponds to the level by which they agree or disagree with a statement that it is the role of the government to do so. Researchers then try to explain how these responses depend on observable characteristics, such as age, marital status, gender, employment status, education and race.[25]

The motivation for this approach was as an empirical test of the median-voter model of income redistribution developed by Meltzer and Richard (1981). This model predicts that the more unequal the underlying distribution of the individual productivity (as measured by the difference in the mean and median of the distribution), the more income redistribution there will be. To see this, consider the linear progressive income tax system discussed previously and assume there

---

[24] See Bourguignon and Spadaro (2012), Bargain et al. (2014a, 2014b) and Jacobs et al. (2017).

[25] Alesina and Giuliano (2011) survey the empirical results for the USA, and Olivera (2015) summarizes results from various European countries.

is a constant labour supply elasticity with no income effects. An individual with productivity w has the indirect utility $v(t, b; w)$ as given by (11). With no income effects, labour supply will be strictly decreasing in the tax rate, and higher$-w$ individuals will provide more labour and earn higher incomes.

Now suppose individuals could choose their preferred tax rates recognizing that the lump-sum transfer b is determined from the government's budget constraint in (12) with a zero revenue requirement ($R = 0$). The individual's preferred tax rate solves

$$\max_t v(t, b; w) \quad \text{s.t.} \quad b = t \int_{\underline{w}}^{\overline{w}} w\ell(t; w)f(w)dw,$$

which yields $t^*(w)$. Utility for a type w, $v(t, b; w)$, is single-peaked, and preferred tax rates $t^*(w)$ are decreasing in w. The highest preferred tax rate will be given by $t^*(\underline{w})$, the lowest by $t^*(\overline{w})$ and the median preferred tax rate by $t^m = t^*(w^m)$, where w^m is the median wage. Consequently, the majority of individuals will support the preferred tax rate of the median wage or equivalently median income individual, and this tax rate will be given by

$$\frac{t^m}{1 - t^m} = \frac{1 - \frac{y^m}{\mathbb{E}(y)}}{\epsilon}.$$

The numerator reflects the difference between the average income and the median income. It is positive when the median income is below the mean and will be larger the higher the mean income is relative to the median income. The denominator is the elasticity of labour supply or equivalently the elasticity of taxable income that would be weighted by income if it were not assumed to be the same for all individuals. The median-voter model then predicts that the size of the government (in terms of the amount of income redistribution) will depend positively on the degree of income inequality.

Existing evidence provides limited support for the median-voter model of income redistribution. This could be due to a failure of the median-voter rule in aggregating social preferences rather than individual preferences for redistribution being unaffected by income inequality. Alesina and Giuliano (2011) have shown that at least in some countries, individual preferences are affected by observed inequality. In the USA, however, evidence from the General Social Survey shows that individuals' stated preferences for redistribution have not been affected by changes in income inequality, even by those with incomes below the mean (Kuziemko et al., 2015). To explore whether this finding is a result of a lack of information about the actual amount of income inequality, Kuziemko et al. use a randomized experimental information survey treatment and find that while stated concern for income inequality increases with information, it does not increase support for government redistributive policies in large part due to mistrust in the government.

Researchers have also examined how individual perceptions about immigration and mobility, or position within the income distribution, affect stated preferences for redistribution. In cross-country analyses, Alesina et al. (2019) find that just asking people about immigration negatively influences their stated preferences for redistribution. Alesina et al. (2018) find a negative correlation between beliefs about the degree of intergenerational mobility and preference for redistribution: the greater the optimism about mobility, the lower the desired redistribution. Using Danish survey data on individuals' perceptions of how their income compares to the income of various reference groups linked to detailed administrative data on individuals' actual income histories, Hvidberg et al. (2020) show that these relative positions matter for how individuals perceive fairness of income inequality. Furthermore, experiencing a negative income shock reduces the perceived fairness of inequality whereas a positive income shock has the opposite effect.

Other interesting work explores whether preferences for redistribution are affected by individual perceptions about (a) whether income (high or low) is largely determined by factors outside or under the control of individuals, that is, "luck" versus "effort" and (b) how deserving potential income transfer recipients are. Examining the perceived determinants of income, findings suggest that the more individuals perceive income being determined by effort, the lower the preference for redistribution (Fong, 2001). This also holds for the perceived relative deservedness of potential income transfer recipients. Those unable to work or unable to find work are perceived to be more deserving of an income transfer than those able to work or not looking for work (Saez and Stantcheva, 2016, Online Appendix C).

Survey findings also suggest that social preferences are not well represented by the standard social welfare functions. In the optimal income tax approach, social welfare depends only on final outcomes and not on the process by which they are obtained or on initial positions. Using a stated-preference experiment, Tarroux (2019) shows that individuals' rankings of different allocations of pre- and post-tax income in terms of fairness depend on the information provided to individuals about the tax function used to obtain the post-tax income allocations from the pre-tax allocations. Survey respondents were shown to place value on the progressivity of average tax rates independent of their impact on the final distribution of income. Weinzierl (2014) also presents survey evidence that shows when placed in the position of a social planner, some individuals will choose a tax system satisfying the principle of equal sacrifice such that everyone gives up the same amount of utility when paying income taxes over a tax system consistent with a utilitarian social welfare function.

These results on social preferences lend mixed support to the social welfare–maximizing approach and point to the importance of some of the conceptual issues mentioned earlier. The optimal inverse approach is consistent with tax policy being based on a Paretian social welfare function with diminishing social welfare weights. At the same time, both approaches support the importance of luck (principle of compensation) versus effort (responsibility) as a rationale for redistribution. For example, social weights tend to be highest for those unemployed. Finally, stated preference findings show that individuals put some weight on equal sacrifice in addition to social welfare as a basis for redistribution.

6 Different Labour Market Environments

In the standard optimal income tax literature, the demand for labour is perfectly elastic so all labour supplied is employed at fixed wage rates. Once labour demand considerations are taken into account, wages may no longer be fixed and employment may no longer be guaranteed. Changes in income taxes and transfers can affect market wages as well as employment, and this can change the optimal income tax structure. Both labour supply and labour demand responses become relevant. First, we discuss the case of endogenous wages. Then we turn to involuntary unemployment and distinguish between the cases where individuals are unable to find work either permanently or temporarily.

6.1 Endogenous Wages

Wages can be endogenous for various reasons. Stiglitz (1982) considered the case where relative wages of different skill types are determined in general equilibrium by their relative supplies. He analyzed the case of two skill types and argued that the marginal tax rate on the high-skilled type should be negative, rather than zero as in the standard analysis. Decreasing the top marginal tax rate encourages the supply of high-skilled workers, which in turn increases the relative wage of low-skilled workers, thereby enhancing redistribution. While Stiglitz's focus was on the top marginal tax rate, similar considerations apply to low-skilled workers. A higher marginal tax rate at the bottom discourages low-skilled labour supply, which increases the low-skilled wage and enhances redistribution. Similarly, a higher participation tax on low-skilled workers in an extensive-margin model should increase the wage payment to them.

Such reasoning suggests that increasing a transfer to the lowest-income workers will discourage their labour supply by an income effect and increase their equilibrium wage rate. This effect is reinforced if the transfer is taxed back. The latter entails a substitution effect that further reduces labour supply and increases the wage rate. Kasy (2018) argues that this favours negative income tax (NIT) with a positive tax back rate relative to the US EITC system where the effective marginal tax rate at the bottom can be very low and possibly negative. Some of the benefits of the EITC accrue to firms whose wage payments are reduced. Rothstein (2010) simulates the effects of the EITC in the USA compared with a standard NIT system. He finds that a large proportion of the EITC accrues to firms through reduced wage payments. A \$1 increase in EITC payments increases recipients' incomes by only \$0.73. Moreover, workers not eligible for the EITC suffer a reduction in incomes due to the EITC-induced fall in wage rates. On the other hand, \$1 spent on the NIT leads to an increase in recipients' incomes of \$1.39 due to the induced increase in wage rates.

Wage rates may also be affected by human capital investment. Bovenberg and Jacobs (2005) and Jacobs and Bovenberg (2010, 2011) have incorporated human capital investment into optimal income tax models. They show that a progressive earnings tax discourages human capital investment since the marginal tax rate is higher on increases in earnings than on forgone earnings resulting from such investment. This effect can be mitigated by subsidizing human capital investment or taxing capital income. Stantcheva (2015) studies the case for subsidizing human capital accumulation in a dynamic optimal income tax analysis. The analysis is complex and shows that the argument for subsidizing individuals' human capital investment depends on the extent to which a subsidy increases wages and therefore labour supply, whether an investment in human capital is complementary with labour supply (learning-and-doing) or substitutable (learning-or-doing) and the differential effect of training on persons of different skill levels. Blumkin and Sadka (2005) analyze the effects of intergenerational mobility on tax progressivity when individuals' wage rates depend on their parent's wage rate and on the level of education, and the government levies a linear progressive tax. They show that optimal tax progressivity falls with mobility, and with inequality if mobility is high enough.

6.2 Involuntary Unemployment

So far, the labour market models described assume that the demand for labour satisfies the supply of labour at the market wage. In this subsection, we explore labour market environments where individuals may be willing and able to work, or to work more hours, at the prevailing market wage, but opportunities are not available to them. In these environments, some workers are either involuntarily unemployed or underemployed. Much of the literature focuses on the former, reflecting the assumption in extensive models of labour supply that workers cannot change their hours of work. Involuntary unemployment can result from labour market inefficiencies, such as matching frictions in a job search or efficiency wages. It can also result from minimum wages that cause excess labour supply.

We consider the implications of involuntary unemployment for the optimal tax-transfer system. There are two dominant effects. First, when all unemployment is voluntary, the optimal transfer to unemployed individuals is constrained by the behavioural response it elicits, such as a reduction in participation or hours of work. For individuals who are willing to work, but for some reason unable, this behavioural response is mitigated, and an income transfer will not change their labour earnings. The more of those not working who are involuntarily unemployed, the less will be the labour market consequences of increased transfers to the unemployed. Changes in the optimal income tax system will affect both the extent of unemployment and the wage obtained by those who have a job. Second, with involuntary unemployment, a transfer to the unemployed takes on an insurance role in addition to a redistributive one. Under these conditions, the optimal transfer is larger than in the case with only voluntary unemployment.

The length of the spell of involuntary unemployment can also affect the role of the transfer to the unemployed. The policy response to short-term involuntary unemployment is unemployment insurance, whereas policy to address long-term unemployment emphasizes redistribution. Temporary lay-offs or frictional unemployment due to job turnover are covered by unemployment insurance and self-insurance. Structural unemployment leading to persistent earnings loss is addressed in part by redistributive policies. Retraining typically results in only partial recovery of earnings loss (Jacobson et al., 1993, 2005). Displaced workers who suffer permanent wage rate declines are comparable to those who have low skills at the outset, so are candidates for optimal income tax policies. An alternative approach to address wage shocks is wage insurance (LaLonde, 2007), though there is limited literature on that.

The normative policy literature has tended to draw a sharp distinction between workers who face permanent unemployment and ought to receive redistributive transfers versus those who are temporarily unemployed and ought to receive unemployment insurance. We follow the literature and deal with permanent and temporary unemployment separately in the following subsections.

6.2.1 Long-Term Involuntary Unemployment

Optimal income tax analyses typically adopt classic dynamic search or matching models (Pissarides, 2000; Rogerson et al., 2005) to explain involuntary unemployment. Static versions of these models are typically used in which individuals make one labour market choice that has permanent consequences. Other models of involuntary unemployment, such as efficiency wages or turnover models, are rarely used.

The key elements of the static matching models are as follows. Consider the market for workers of a given skill type. Firms seeking to hire workers of this type post vacancies, where there is a fixed cost per vacancy posted. Once hired, workers produce output according to a concave production function. Firms are competitive and are free to enter or exit. A zero-expected profit condition determines the number of firms and therefore the total number of vacancies posted, V. Unemployed workers of each skill-type search for jobs for their type. The total number of workers of a given type searching is U. A matching function, $M(U, V)$, with $M_U(U, V) > 0$ and $M_V(U, V) > 0$, determines the number of positions filled. The matching function is often assumed to be linear homogeneous, so $M(U, V) = VM(1/\theta, 1)$, where $\theta = V/U$ is an index of market tightness. Jobs are filled randomly, so the probability of filling a job is given by $M(U, V)/V = M(1/\theta, 1) \equiv \pi(\theta)$, where $\pi(\theta)$ is decreasing in θ. The probability of a worker obtaining a job is $M(U, V)/U = \theta\pi(\theta)$, which is increasing in θ.

The wage payment y – or earnings, since labour supply is fixed – is determined by bargaining between the worker and the firm after a match has been obtained. (Alternatively, competitive wage-setting will yield similar results, where firms post wages that they will pay for filled vacancies.) With Nash bargaining, the equilibrium wage maximizes the Nash product of the surpluses of workers and firms, $(y - T(y) - b)^\rho (a - y)^{1-\rho}$, where $T(y)$ is the earnings tax function, b is the transfer to the unemployed, a is the productivity of the worker, and ρ is the relative bargaining power of workers. Bargaining is efficient in the sense that the externalities of search are internalized if the so-called Hosios condition is satisfied. Suppose the matching function takes the Cobb–Douglas form, $M(U, V) = U^\alpha V^{1-\alpha}$. Hosios (1990) showed that if $\rho = \alpha$, the share of the surplus captured by workers in the bargaining process reflects worker's relative productivity at generating matches, and similarly for firms, so that workers' search effort and firms' decisions to create vacancies are efficient. Then, as Lehmann et al. (2011) show, the wage under Nash bargaining maximizes the expected surplus of workers, $\theta\pi(\theta)(y - T(y) - b)$. When workers differ in skills, it is often assumed that this wage bargaining process applies separately to each skill type. While this simplifies the analysis of the optimal tax-transfer system, it restricts workers from searching for jobs of their skill type.

Hungerbühler et al. (2006) were the first to analyze the consequences of involuntary unemployment for optimal income taxation. They adopt an extensive-margin model in which workers choose whether to seek a job at their skill level, and job search success depends on the skill-specific matching technology. The value of leisure is the same for all regardless of skills. This leads to a cutoff skill level $\tilde{a}$ such that workers participate if and only if $a \geq \tilde{a}$. For those who obtain a job, wage earnings y are determined by Nash wage bargaining, which is efficient since the Hosios condition is satisfied. The government observes earnings y and chooses a non-linear income tax $T(y)$ to maximize a social welfare function with inequality aversion subject to a budget constraint and incentive constraints. Since the government cannot distinguish the voluntary from the involuntarily unemployed, it pays the same transfer b to all. While the government observes employment earnings y, it cannot observe worker abilities a. This implies that firms employing workers of one skill level can mimic the bargaining outcomes of others. To preclude this, an incentive constraint applies to wage bargains, which along with the endogenous participation decision constrains government redistribution policies.

The tax structure $T(y)$ affects both bargaining outcomes y and the cutoff skill level $\tilde{a}$ determining participation. In particular, participation is decreasing in the average tax rate $T(y)/y$. At the same time, the tax affects the wage determined by bargaining in conflicting ways. An increase in total tax liabilities $T(y)$ reduces worker's surplus, thereby causing an increase in wages and a decrease in employment. An increase in the marginal tax rate $T'(y)$ reduces the incentive for workers to bargain for higher wages. Hence, wages fall and employment rises. Unlike in Saez (2002), the participation tax applying to the marginal participant is always positive. The marginal income tax rate $T'(y)$ is positive for all y, while the average tax rate $T(y)/y$ is increasing. Numerical simulations indicate that marginal tax rates are much higher than in the Mirrlees model.

Some of the restrictive assumptions of Hungerbühler et al. (2006) have been relaxed in the subsequent literature. Lehmann et al. (2011) allow heterogeneity in the value of leisure at all skill levels. This leads to both voluntary and involuntary unemployment for all skill types. Variable participation at each skill level creates a participation elasticity as in Saez (2002), which makes comparison with the latter possible. Lehmann et al. first consider the maximin case, where the least well-off are the involuntarily unemployed who all receive the same transfer. Optimal marginal tax rates are positive everywhere and tend to be higher than in models with no involuntary unemployment. Participation tax rates are positive everywhere, as in the pure extensive-margin case under maximin. If the elasticity of participation falls with the skill level, which is plausible, then the average tax rate is increasing in earnings. When social welfare exhibits finite inequality aversion, analytical solutions are not possible, and Lehmann et al. resort to simulations. In this case, the participation tax and the marginal tax rate can be negative at the bottom as in Saez (2002).

Jacquet et al. (2014) analyze a variant of Lehmann et al. (2011). They rule out the possibility of one skill level mimicking another by choosing the same wage, and they assume wage bargaining takes the form of Kalai bargaining rather than Nash bargaining. The latter implies that the shares of the surplus accruing to workers and firms are exogenously fixed. Earnings of a type$-a$ worker are $y_a = \rho_a a + (1 - \rho_a)(T(y_a) - b)$, where ρ_a is the proportion of the surplus from the bargain accruing to workers.[26] This implies that the equilibrium wage is increasing in the level of the tax and does not depend on the marginal tax rate. An increase in the tax on a given skill level both reduces labour demand – since y increases – and reduces labour supply – since participation decreases.

Using this, the optimal participation tax for workers of skill level a is a straightforward extension of (22) of the pure extensive-margin case:

$$\frac{T(y_a) + b}{c_a - c_0} = \frac{1 - g_a \rho_a \left(1 + \eta_a^D\right)}{\rho_a \left(\eta_a^D + \eta_a^P + \eta_a^D \eta_a^P\right)},$$

where η_a^P is the elasticity of participation and η_a^D is the elasticity of demand for a type$-a$ worker with respect to the surplus accruing to the firm, $a - y_a$. This makes it clear that there are both demand and supply influences at work in labour matching models. Jacquet et al. (2013) simulate the optimal values of participation tax rates using values for the elasticities η_a^P and η_a^D that are empirically reasonable. They find that optimal taxes are systematically lower than in pure extensive-margin models without involuntary unemployment, which is intuitive since there is now an additional decision margin influenced by the tax. They also find that the optimal employment tax decreases when the elasticity of labour demand increases relative to the participation elasticity.

Kroft et al. (2020) build on Lehmann et al. (2011) by developing a sufficient statistic approach to formulating the tax structure. Individuals face a distribution of occupation-specific discrete search costs and decide whether to search for work in a particular occupation. Wages/output are observable, and income tax liabilities are occupation-specific. Search activity is unobservable, so transfers

---

[26] More precisely, the wage rate y for type$-a$ maximizes the minimum of $(y - T(y) - b)/\rho_a$ and $(a - y)/(1 - \rho_a)$ so ρ_a is the bargaining strength of the worker.

to both the voluntary unemployed (those not searching for work) and the involuntarily unemployed (those unable to find work) are the same. They do not specify how wages and employment are determined. Instead, they simply assume that the equilibrium distribution of wages and employment across occupations depends on the government's tax policies. Employment in an occupation equals the product of the number of workers who search for a job in that occupation and the conditional probability that a participant will find a job.

Kroft et al. (2020) differentiate between micro and macro responses to taxes. Micro responses reflect changes in occupational participation decisions arising from heterogeneous search costs across possible occupations, given wages and conditional probabilities of employment. Macro responses represent the general equilibrium changes in wages and conditional probabilities of employment. The optimal tax formula depends on both micro and macro responses.

This is most easily seen in the pure extensive-margin case where individuals only search for work in one occupation. The macro effects of a tax change are restricted to effects of the wage and conditional probability of employment in a given occupation. The optimal participation tax is a straightforward extension of (22):

$$\frac{T_i + c_0}{c_i - c_0} = \frac{1 - g_i(\phi_i^M / \phi_i^m)}{\eta_i},$$

where the new terms on the right-hand side are the macro participation elasticity ϕ_i^M, the macro employment elasticity η_i that captures changes in both participation and conditional probabilities and the micro participation elasticity ϕ_i^m.

Kroft et al. (2020) define g_i as the social welfare weight of giving individuals in occupation i one more dollar holding wages and conditional probabilities fixed as in Saez (2002). Since this additional dollar results in general equilibrium effects, g_i is multiplied by the ratio of the macro to micro participation elasticities. With fixed wages and full employment, the participation tax reduces to (22) since with fixed conditional probabilities of employment η_i will be equal to ϕ_i^M, and with fixed wages, the micro and macro participation elasticities will be the same.

Having a negative participation tax rate at the bottom of the earnings distribution now depends on whether g_1 is greater than the ratio of the macro to the micro participation elasticity (ϕ_1^M / ϕ_1^m). The size of this ratio depends on the assumed underlying wage determination process and could be greater or less than one. In the case of risk-neutral individuals and the search/matching model discussed previously, the ratio will be less (greater) than one if the workers' bargaining power is greater (less) than the elasticity of the matching function and will be equal to one if the Hosios condition is satisfied. Notably, the equity effect of an increase in the tax rate depends on general equilibrium responses of wages and conditional probabilities, while for efficiency what matters is the macro response of employment. Similarly, in the case when individuals can also choose to work in one of two adjacent occupations, changes in taxes in one occupation can have spillover effects on wages and employment in other occupations, and the optimal tax rule would be modified accordingly.

The papers discussed so far assume that the government does not distinguish between the voluntary and involuntarily unemployed and makes the same transfer to each. Boadway and Cuff (2014) assume that the government can instead observe imperfectly those who are involuntarily unemployed using an unspecified monitoring mechanism. More intensive monitoring increases the difference between transfers to the voluntary and involuntarily unemployed and increases the transfer to the voluntary unemployed.[27]

Another source of involuntary unemployment is excess labour supply as a result of minimum wages. Much of the focus of the optimal tax literature has been on determining whether a minimum wage can be a complementary policy tool to the optimal income tax. Boadway and Cuff (2001) demonstrate in the standard non-linear income tax model that if the government can perfectly monitor job search/offers and requires all job offers to be accepted, then with a binding minimum wage, only individuals with abilities greater than the minimum wage will be offered jobs. Consequently, the government has information about the abilities of those who are not working and can provide a higher transfer to them. Other papers have focused on economies where wages are determined endogenously. In such a setting with intensive-margin labour decisions, Marceau and Boadway (1994) demonstrate that a minimum wage inducing involuntary unemployment of low-skilled workers can improve social welfare if the low-skilled have a negative tax liability. Lee and Saez (2012) obtain a similar result in a model in which individuals make participation decisions and differ in their cost of working in one of two possible occupations. They assume efficient rationing so that unemployment induced by a minimum wage will affect those with the highest costs of working. Then, a minimum wage in the low-skilled occupation can be welfare improving if participation in this occupation is being subsidized. A minimum wage can mitigate positive labour

---

[27] Different approaches to monitoring in transfer schemes may be found in Boadway and Cuff (1999, 2014), Kleven and Kopczuk (2011) and Boone and Bovenberg (2013).

supply/participation distortions induced by the optimal income tax system and enhance redistribution to the low-skilled.

Other papers have considered settings in which there is temporary involuntary unemployment and a minimum wage policy can have redistributive and efficiency-enhancing roles. In Hungerbühler and Lehmann (2009), there is wage bargaining between workers and firms, and the bargaining share of workers is assumed to be less than the elasticity of the matching function, so the Hosios condition is violated and bargaining is inefficient. A binding minimum wage at the bottom of the wage distribution can be welfare-improving. Similarly, Lavecchia (2020) shows that a minimum wage can reduce search congestion externalities. He also shows that without search frictions if the optimal participation tax is negative for the lowest-skill occupation, then imposing a minimum wage offsets this distortion and results in greater redistribution.

6.2.2 Temporary Involuntary Unemployment

When involuntary unemployment is temporary, a transfer to the unemployed acts more as a form of unemployment insurance than a redistributive transfer (although it is also that). A targeted transfer would act as an income-tested form of unemployment insurance, where workers with lower wealth and lower wages – and therefore less ability to self-insure – would receive a higher transfer. Similar search models as in the permanent unemployment case are used here except they must be dynamic, where individuals make choices each period and can transition from one job to another. Depending on the model, this may lead them to choose to hold off accepting a job if they believe a better one can be found by waiting. Alternatively, in models where it is relatively easy to find a job once you already have one, individuals may accept jobs they would not in a static search model. In dynamic search models, an unemployment transfer can affect job turnover, the duration of search, and search intensity. Given that unemployment is temporary, explaining job loss should be part of the analysis. However, in much of the literature, that is not done. Sometimes, job loss is simply assumed to be random.

The literature on optimal unemployment insurance has largely ignored any redistributive role and focused on efficiency concerns. Although studies of the design of unemployment insurance have been around a long time (see Karni, 1999), the recent literature has been inspired by Chetty (2008). He considers a representative-individual model in which the individual faces some chance of becoming unemployed. The individual can respond by searching for work if unemployed and self-insuring against the income loss due to unemployment. In the absence of full self-insurance (or a private unemployment insurance market), government-provided unemployment insurance serves to smooth consumption between employment and unemployment but discourages search. Optimal unemployment insurance trades off these two effects. Chetty considers both a static and a dynamic model in which the duration of unemployment spells depends on search.

Landais et al. (2018) augment the model of Chetty (2008) by assuming unemployment is determined by a standard matching technology with wages determined by bargaining. With matching models, labour market tightness (the ratio of vacancies to job-seekers) is endogenous and may be inefficient because wage bargaining is inefficient. In this context, optimal unemployment insurance involves not just a trade-off between insurance and search effort but also a correction for inefficient market tightness. If labour market tightness is too low because bargaining leads to excessive wages, unemployment insurance should be lowered to increase tightness, and vice versa. Landais et al. argue that since tightness falls during recessions, unemployment insurance should rise. Spinnewijn (2015) finds that the unemployed overestimate their chances of getting a job, so they search and save too little. To correct for these behavioural biases, unemployment benefits should be appropriately higher.

These models assess unemployment insurance using efficiency criteria. Boadway and Cuff (2018) consider an extensive-margin optimal income tax setting with search unemployment in which unemployment insurance transfers exist alongside transfers to the voluntary unemployed. Workers are risk-averse, but they are unable to insure themselves against income losses if involuntarily unemployed. They can choose to be voluntarily unemployed or to search for a job in which case they decide how much search effort to exert. The government observes whether workers search or not, but it cannot observe their type if unemployed. For those who obtain a job match, the government observes both the output they produce and the wages they obtain by bargaining. The government imposes a piecewise linear income tax such that workers of different wages face different marginal tax rates and lump-sum transfers. The government sets a separate transfer to the voluntary and involuntarily unemployed, where the latter is equivalent to an unemployment insurance benefit.

The Boadway–Cuff model includes both insurance and redistribution concerns, possible inefficiencies of search and wage-setting and individual participation and search effort decisions. Government social welfare maximization leads to assigning different policy instruments to different policy targets. Marginal wage tax rates affect bargained wage rates and are chosen to achieve efficient wage-setting. This implies that in its choices of transfers to employed workers of different types (i.e., average tax rates) and to the voluntary and involuntarily unemployed, the government need not take account of their effects on wage rates. The optimal unemployment benefit trades off insurance with participation and search incentives but is independent of equity weights. Optimal redistribution is achieved by type-specific transfers (average tax rates) to the employed and transfers to the voluntary unemployed and is constrained by both participation and search decisions. Overall, these results provide justification for separating unemployment insurance design from the redistributive tax-transfer policy. The assumptions of the analysis are however demanding, and more work needs to be done since, in the real world, policy instruments cannot be so finely targeted.

7 Behavioural Economics Considerations

Behavioural economics studies economic outcomes and policies when individuals do not behave as well-informed, rational, self-interested agents. Individual decisions might exhibit present bias if they put excessive weight on current versus future benefits or costs. The result can be undersaving, procrastination or unhealthy consumption choices. Individuals may be hampered by bounded rationality and rely on rules of thumb, heuristics or other arbitrary decision rules. They may be inattentive and not take proper account of available information, or their choices might be influenced by considerations irrelevant to the underlying economic decision or to the manner in which choices are framed. They may also make choices against their own interest because they are motivated by moral considerations or by social norms.

Our concern is how behavioural economic considerations influence optimal income tax policies. An important conceptual issue that arises in designing policies in these circumstances is the legitimacy of the government overriding the preferences of individuals to correct their behaviour. There is a limited literature on this, and it typically regards government intervention as legitimate on the grounds that the government is taking the long-run interests of individuals into account.

We begin with brief discussions of interdependent utilities and social norms since these influence individual behaviour in ways that are potentially important for redistribution policies. We then consider the design of optimal linear and non-linear income taxes in light of behavioural biases.

7.1 Social Norms

Social norms can be understood as the propensities of individuals to take actions out of an intrinsic desire to follow societal norms of behaviour independent of individual utility, where the propensities are shared by a population (Elster, 1989). Such norms have been shown to be particularly important in the context of tax compliance, and there is increasing evidence they also matter for individual work decisions.[28]

Aronsson and Sjögren (2010) incorporate norms regarding both extensive and intensive work decisions in examining Pareto efficient income taxation in a two-ability-type optimal income tax model. The intensive social norm is modelled as a utility cost if hours worked deviate from some reference number of hours (either the mean or the mode of the hours-worked distribution). This generates a potential wedge between an individual's marginal rate of substitution of leisure for consumption and their after-tax wage. Consequently, from the planner's perspective (who respects individual preferences), working generates an externality that can be corrected through the income tax system. The form of corrective taxation (positive or negative marginal tax rates) ultimately depends on the distribution of ability types in the population since this determines the distribution of hours worked and the reference hours.

To capture the extensive, or participation, social norm, Aronsson and Sjögren assume the utility cost of not participating depends positively on the total number of participants in the population. The participation (extensive) social norm alone does not change the Pareto efficient income tax schedule relative to the case without any social norms, since the optimal marginal tax rates depend only on the intensive labour supply decisions. The optimal marginal tax rates will be affected by the presence of social norms relating to hours worked depending on the reference hours (intensive social norms). The optimal tax changes to address the externalities arising from the intensive margin norms will also affect individuals' participation decisions.

Boadway and Martineau (2016) instead focus on social norms affecting the work participation decisions using the extensive-margin model of Diamond (1980) and Saez (2002). They assume the participation decision for a type$-i$ individual is given by

---

[28] Various papers have demonstrated that individuals' tax compliance is affected by information or beliefs about other taxpayer's compliance behaviour. See Alm et al. (1999) and Wenzel (2005), and the survey in Luttmer and Singhal (2014). Kleven (2014) explores social norms as an explanation for the observed high levels of taxation in Norway, Sweden and Denmark relative to the United States. For evidence that labour supply depends on social norms, see Woittiez and Kapteyn (1998), Aronsson et al. (1999) and Grodner and Kniesner (2006).

$$c_i + x(h_0, c_0) \geq c_0 + \delta_i,$$

where c_i is consumption if working, c_0 is the transfer if not working and δ_i is the utility from leisure. The term $x(h_0, c_0)$ is a social norm term reflecting the moral reward of work, where h_0 is the total number of non-participants. Low levels of non-participation h_0 indicate that most non-participants not working due to luck rather than choice, and vice versa for high values of h_0. For low values of h_0, $x(\cdot)$ is positive and increasing in the transfer to non-participants, while the opposite is true for high values of h_0. Social norms may also affect the utility cost of not participating (which can be viewed as a form of stigma). The size of optimal participation taxes depends on the welfare weight given to non-participants and on the strength of the feedback effects of the social norm on participation and government resources. Multiple local stable equilibria can arise, where the optimal tax at a point in time is constrained by present social norms, but governments could also use the tax system to induce a change in norms.

As Boadway and Martineau discuss, the transition dynamics of shifting from one equilibrium to another (e.g., from a low participation to high participation economy) are complex and depend on political factors. For example, if a government initiates but does not complete a transition from one equilibrium to another for some reason (such as losing power or an electoral backlash), individuals may end up being worse off. If, however, commitment to a complete transition is possible, transitioning from one equilibrium to another has the potential to be Pareto improving. Focusing on a local equilibrium with a low (high) level of non-participation, the participation social norm will result in higher (lower) optimal participation taxes than without the social norm.

7.2 Optimal Income Taxation with Behavioural Biases

Behavioural considerations have been incorporated into optimal income tax models by Gerritsen (2016), Lockwood (2020), Bernheim and Taubinsky (2018) and Farhi and Gabaix (2020). In each case, deviations from standard behaviour take the form of biases in labour choice. Consider the case of a linear progressive income tax, $T(y) = ty - b$. Suppose the utility function takes the quasilinear form $u(c - h(\ell))$. In the absence of bias, an individual with wage rate w solves problem (11) giving

$$h'(\ell) = (1 - t)w, \quad \Rightarrow \quad \ell((1 - t)w) \tag{26}$$

and the indirect utility function $v(t, b; w)$. For individuals with behavioural bias, (26) is not satisfied. Following Gerritsen (2016), define the bias by σ, where

$$\sigma = \frac{h'(\ell)}{(1-t)w} - 1.$$

The bias could represent various behavioural considerations discussed previously, such as present bias, keeping up with the "Jones" and so on. If $\sigma > 0$, the individual supplies too much labour, and vice versa. In Bernheim and Taubinsky (2018), σ varies among wage types, and we denote it σ_w.

The government treats σ_w as a deviation from optimal behaviour with no weight in social welfare. The government maximizes a utilitarian social welfare function $\int v(t, b; w)dF(w)$ subject to an aggregate budget constraint $b = \int ty(w)dF(w) = t\bar{y}$, where $\bar{y}$ is average income. The problem is a straightforward extension of the standard optimal linear progressive taxation problem discussed previously, and the optimal tax rate t is an extension of (15):

$$\frac{t}{1-t} = -\frac{\text{Cov}[\beta(w), y(w)]}{\bar{\beta}\bar{y}\varepsilon_{\bar{y}}} + (\text{E}[\sigma_w] + \text{Cov}[\sigma_w, \nu(w)]), \qquad (27)$$

where $\varepsilon_{y(w)}$ is the elasticity of taxable income, $\beta(w)$ is the net marginal social value of income as defined previously in (14) and $\nu(w) = \beta(w)y\varepsilon_{y(w)}/(\bar{\beta}\bar{y}\varepsilon_{\bar{y}})$ reflects how the taxpayer's marginal utility of consumption and elasticity of taxable income compare with the average. Equation (27) differs from the standard case by the last term, which reflects the social benefit from offsetting individual biases. If $\sigma_w > 0$, the tax rate is increased to reduce the oversupply of labour. The correction will be greater to the extent that those with large biases have higher marginal utilities of consumption and elasticities of taxable income.

Bernheim and Taubinsky (2018) also consider the case where the bias is due to misperceptions about the tax rate. If individuals underestimate the income tax rate, they are less responsive to increases in the tax rate. This allows the government to set a higher tax rate and achieve more redistribution.

Lockwood (2020) assumes that behavioural distortion takes the form of present bias. Consumers put excessive weight on labour supply relative to consumption and maximize the biased utility function $u((1 + \sigma_w)c - h(\ell))$, where $\sigma_w < 0$. Their first-order condition is $h'(\ell) = (1 + \sigma_w)(1 - t)w$, so they undersupply labour. Assuming σ_w is the same for all, (27) reduces to

$$\frac{t}{1-t} = -\frac{\text{Cov}[\beta(w), y(w)]}{\bar{\beta}\bar{y}\varepsilon_{\bar{y}}} + \sigma.$$

The smaller is σ, that is, the greater is the present bias, the more is labour undersupplied and the lower is the optimal marginal tax rate.

This analysis has been extended to optimal non-linear income taxation by Gerritsen (2016) and Farhi and Gabaix (2020). The approach of Fahri and Gabaix extends that of Bernheim and Taubinsky by incorporating additional behavioural effects. Suppose we write the utility function in terms of consumption and income as $v(c, y; w) \equiv u(c, y/w)$. Maximizing this subject to the budget constraint $c = y - T(y)$ gives the first-order condition $(1 - T'(y))v_c + v_y = 0$. Drawing on Gerritsen (2016), Fahri and Gabaix define the behavioural wedge as

$$\tau^b(y) = -\frac{\left(1 - T'(y)\right)v_c + v_y}{v_b},$$

where v_b is the marginal utility of income. If $\tau^b(y) > 0$, the individual overestimates the benefits of working and works too much, and vice versa. This definition captures the individual's misoptimization over the labour supply discussed above.

A second behavioural effect considered in Fahri and Gavaix is referred to as a behaviour cross-influence, denoted $\epsilon_{y^*}(y)$. It is the compensated elasticity of earnings of an individual of income y with respect to the marginal retention rate at income level $y^* \neq y$, that is, $(1 - T'(y^*))$. For example, if individuals mistakenly treat average tax rates as marginal tax rates, the tax rate at $y^* < y$ influences labour supply at income level y, and $\epsilon_{y^*}(y) > 0$. Fahri and Gavaix derive the optimal marginal tax rate analogous to (19) in the presence of these two behavioural effects:

$$\frac{T'(y^*) - \tilde{\tau}^b(y^*)}{1 - T'(y^*)}$$
$$= \frac{\left(1 - H(y^*)\right)\left(1 - G(y^*)\right)}{\epsilon(y^*)y^*h(y^*)} - \int_0^\infty \frac{\epsilon_{y^*}(y)}{\epsilon(y^*)} \frac{T'(y) - \tilde{\tau}^b(y)}{1 - T'(y)} \frac{yh(y)}{y^*h(y^*)} dy.$$
$$(28)$$

The first term on the right-hand side is the same as in the standard case of (19). The other terms capture behavioural effects. When the behavioural cross-influence elasticity $\epsilon_{y^*}(y)$ is positive, an increase in the tax rate of individuals at income y^* causes those at income y to perceive their own tax rates as higher, leading to a decrease in the labour supply and a reduction in the optimal marginal tax rate. The tax rate is also affected by the behavioural wedge, $\tilde{\tau}^b(y)$, caused by misperceptions of the value of working. When $\tilde{\tau}^b(y) > 0$, the agent works too much, and the optimal marginal tax rate will increase.

Fahri and Gabaix note that when $\tilde{\tau}^b(y) < 0$, it is possible that $T'(y^*) < 0$. For example, individuals may underestimate the fact that more working leads to higher human capital accumulation and higher wages in the future. They argue that these biases could be particularly important at the bottom of the earnings distribution leading to negative marginal tax rates at low incomes. This would provide a behavioural rationale for an EITC that is different from the rationale offered by Saez (2002).

Gerritsen (2016) derives the analogue of (27) without the behavioural cross-influence, so $\epsilon_{y^*}(y) = 0$. He empirically estimates the behaviour wedge $\tilde{\tau}^b(y)$, which is a sufficient statistic for the degree of individual misoptimization. He uses information on life satisfaction from the British Household Panel Survey as a measure of individual well-being based on respondents' answers to the question whether they would prefer to work fewer, greater or the same number of hours at their current hourly wage rate. He finds support for a positive relationship between a worker's current income and the amount they are working relative to their well-being maximizing amount. Consequently, the marginal tax rates on low-income individuals should be lower to induce greater labour supply, lending some empirical support to the assertion of Fahri and Gabaix.

8 Summary of Policy Implications

The intent of the optimal tax literature is to inform tax policy choices. The approach is abstract and emphasizes the broad features of the economy and of individual choices at the expense of details. Nonetheless, some persuasive policy prescriptions emerge that have influenced governments and their policy advisors in recent years. Mirrlees et al. (2011), for example, relies to a considerable extent on the optimal tax approach. We summarize some of the main proposals that have originated in the optimal tax approach. Our examples rely mainly on the aspects of the literature that space constraints have allowed us to pursue. Some topics that we have neglected but that are addressed elsewhere in the literature are mentioned at the end. The following is a non-exhaustive list of the policy implications of the optimal tax analysis we have reviewed in this Element.

8.1 Commodity taxation

The Atkinson–Stiglitz theorem and its extension by Laroque (2005) and Kaplow (2006) support a uniform commodity tax structure. Even if weak separability is not strictly satisfied, the administrative costs of imposing differential taxes on some commodities probably outweigh the social welfare gain. There may be some cases where goods are sufficiently complementary with labour to justify special treatment. An example might be childcare that could be subsidized outside the income tax system. There is a strong case for implementing commodity taxes using a VAT. Under a VAT, input tax crediting ensures that no tax applies to intermediate inputs so the production efficiency is retained. Efficiency arguments also support designing business taxes as taxes on economic profits or rents. A cash-flow business tax would accomplish this.

8.2 Income tax base

Intertemporal optimal income tax analysis supports including both labour and capital income in the tax base, regardless of whether the weak separability condition of the Atkinson–Stiglitz Theorem is satisfied. Taxing capital income serves a useful redistribution purpose when propensities to save the increase in wage rates and when wage rates are uncertain and cannot be insured. As well, present bias, and therefore undersaving, likely applies more strongly for lower-income persons. The optimal tax rate on capital income is likely below that of labour income, thereby lending support to a dual income tax system. A strong case can be made on equity grounds for including inheritances in the tax base, either as part of the income tax or as a separate tax. Inheritances represent windfall gains to recipients and result in persistent wealth inequality. The optimal inheritance tax rate depends on efficiency effects as well as costs of collection and compliance, and it may differ from income tax rates (Cremer and Pestieau, 2011).

8.3 Rate structure

The progressivity of the income tax depends on the trade-off between equity and efficiency, and this can differ according to circumstances. Nonetheless, optimal income tax analysis supports some characteristics of the rate structure. Simulations suggest that the rate structure should exhibit relatively high and decreasing marginal tax rates at the bottom, followed by mildly increasing tax rates as incomes rise further. Marginal tax rates could be relatively high in the top tax bracket. Average tax rates should rise throughout the income distribution. If participation elasticities are relatively important at the bottom, a participation subsidy, or earnings subsidy, at low-income levels can be welfare improving. The case for a participation subsidy is also supported by behavioural arguments, although the importance of intensive labour supply responses reduces the case for participation subsidies. Behavioural economics considerations also suggest that individuals may supply too much labour, in which case the efficiency cost of marginal tax rates is reduced.

8.4 Transfers to the unemployed

Individuals who are unemployed may choose not to work, may be unable to work or may be unable to find a job. Optimal income tax analysis supports a transfer to those not working, but the size of the transfer can vary depending on the reason for unemployment. If the government could perfectly distinguish the voluntary from the involuntarily unemployed, it could choose different transfers to the various groups. For those who are temporarily involuntarily unemployed, unemployment insurance would apply and would be based on insurance principles. Unemployment insurance would smooth the income of the involuntarily unemployed by replacing their foregone earnings, but moral hazard effects would rule out full insurance. The transfer to the long-term involuntarily unemployed would be based more on equity considerations, and as long as recipients were searching for work, they would receive a reasonable transfer. For those who are able to find a job but choose not to, difficult equity considerations apply. Even if the equity judgment is favourable, the size of the subsidy is constrained by the disincentive to participate. As we have already seen, a higher participation elasticity calls for a participation subsidy that can lead to a lower transfer to those who choose not to participate. The policy problem becomes more difficult if the government is not able to distinguish perfectly between those able and unable to work and whether those not working are searching for a job. The government has an incentive to improve its information by screening transfer applicants to determine their disability status and by monitoring them ex post to verify that they are actively searching.

8.5 Further issues

There are many more important tax policy issues that space has precluded us from examining. A partial list of them would include environmental taxation, family taxation, business taxation and the taxation of risky returns, specific excise taxation to deter undesirable consumption, tax evasion, international tax competition, the use of in-kind transfers to achieve equity objectives and the taxation of voluntary transfers including charitable donations and bequests. There are also approaches following different methodologies than normative tax analysis. Our analysis has emphasized the choice of an optimal tax system or tax design. There is a large literature on tax reform, that is, the evaluation of small tax changes starting from a non-optimal system. The theorem of Corlett and Hague (1953) was a tax reform analysis that studied the welfare effect of small revenue-neutral changes to the commodity tax structure starting from uniform taxes. The extensions of Laroque (2005), Kaplow (2006) and Hellwig (2010) of the Atkinson–Stiglitz theorem involved studying discrete reforms from non-uniform to uniform commodity taxation combined with revenue-neutral reforms to income taxation. The marginal cost of public funds is a tax reform concept that expresses the change in social welfare from an incremental change in a tax rate. A survey of this concept is found in Dahlby (2008), and an application of it to entire tax systems may be found in Ahmad and Stern (1984). The reader is referred there for more details.

References

Ahmad, Ehtisham and Nicholas Stern (1984), *The Theory and Practice of Tax Reform in Developing Countries* (Cambridge: Cambridge University Press).

Akerlof, George (1978), 'The Economics of "Tagging" as Applied to the Optimal Income Tax, Welfare Programs, and Manpower Training,' *American Economic Review* 68, 8–19.

Ales, Laurence, Musab Kurnaz and Christopher Sleet (2015), 'Technical Change, Wage Inequality, and Taxes,' *American Economic Review* 105, 3061–101.

Alesina, Alberto and Paola Giuliano (2011), 'Preferences for Redistribution,' in A. Bisin and J. Benhabib (eds.), *Handbook of Social Economics* (The Netherlands: North Holland), 93–132.

Alesina, Alberto, Armando Miano and Stefanie Stantcheva (2019), 'Immigration and Redistribution,' NBER Working Paper No. 24733.

Alesina, Alberto, Stefanie Stantcheva and Edoardo Teso (2018), 'Intergenerational Mobility and Preferences for Redistribution,' *American Economic Review* 108, 521–54.

Alm, James, Gary H. McClelland and William D. Schulze (1999), 'Changing the Social Norm of Tax Compliance by Voting,' *Kyklos* 52, 141–71.

Apps, Patricia, Ngo Van Long and Ray Rees (2014), 'Optimal Piecewise Linear Income Taxation,' *Journal of Public Economic Theory* 16(4), 523–45.

Aronsson, Thomas, Sören Blomquist and Hans Sacklén (1999), 'Identifying Interdependent Behaviour in an Empirical Model of Labour Supply,' *Journal of Applied Econometrics* 14, 607–26.

Aronsson, Thomas and Tomas Sjögren (2010), 'Optimal Income Taxation and Social Norms in the Labor Market,' *International Tax and Public Finance* 17, 67–89.

Arrow, Kenneth J. (1951), *Social Choice and Individual Values* (New York: Wiley).

Atkinson, Anthony B. and Joseph E. Stiglitz (1976), 'The Design of Tax Structure: Direct vs. Indirect Taxation,' *Journal of Public Economics* 6, 55–75.

Auerbach, Alan, Michael Devereux and Helen Simpson (2010), 'Taxing Corporate Income,' in S. Adam, T. Besley, R. Blundell et al. (eds.), *Dimensions of Tax Design* (Oxford: Oxford University Press), 838–93.

Australian Treasury (2010), *Australia's Future Tax System* (The Henry Review) (Canberra: Commonwealth of Australia).

Banks, James and Peter Diamond (2010), 'The Base for Direct Taxation,' in S. Adam, T. Besley, R. Blundell et al. (eds.), *Dimensions of Tax Design: The Mirrlees Review* (Oxford: Oxford University Press), 548–648.

Bargain, Olivier, Mathias Dolls, Drik Neumann, Andreas Peichl and Sebastian Siegloch (2014a), 'Tax-Benefit Revealed Social Preferences in Europe and the US,' *Annals of Economics and Statistics* 113/114, 257–89.

Bargain, Olivier, Mathias Dolls, Dirk Neumann, Andreas Peichl and Sebastian Siegloch (2014b), 'Comparing Inequality Aversion across Countries when Labor Supply Responses Differ,' *International Tax and Public Finance* 21, 845–73.

Bastani, Spencer, Sören Blomquist and Luca Micheletto (2019), 'Nonlinear and Piecewise Linear Income Taxation, and the Subsidization of Work-Related Goods,' *International Tax and Public Finance* 26, 806–34.

Bastani, Spencer and Jacob Lundberg (2017), 'Political Preferences for Redistribution in Sweden,' *The Journal of Economic Inequality* 15, 345–67.

Bernheim, B. Douglas and Dmitry Taubinsky (2018), 'Behavioral Public Economics,' in B. D. Bernheim, S. DellaVigna and D. Laibson (eds.), *Handbook of Behavioral Economics*, Volume 1 (Amsterdam: North Holland), 381–516.

Blackorby, Charles and David Donaldson (1988), 'Cash versus Kind, Self Selection and Efficient Transfers,' *American Economic Review* 78, 691–700.

Blumkin, Tomer and Efraim Sadka (2005), 'Income Taxation with Intergenerational Mobility: Can Higher Inequality Lead to Less Progression?' *European Economic Review* 49, 1915–25.

Boadway, Robin (2012), *From Optimal Tax Theory to Tax Policy: Retrospective and Prospective Views*, The Munich Lectures, 2009 (Cambridge, MA: MIT Press).

Boadway, Robin and Neil Bruce (1984), *Welfare Economics* (Oxford: Blackwell).

Boadway, Robin and Katherine Cuff (1999), 'Monitoring Job Search as an Instrument for Targeting Transfers,' *International Tax and Public Finance* 6, 317–37.

Boadway, Robin and Katherine Cuff (2001), 'A Minimum Wage can be Welfare-Improving and Employment-Enhancing,' *European Economic Review* 45, 553–76.

Boadway, Robin and Katherine Cuff (2014), 'Monitoring and Optimal Income Taxation with Involuntary Unemployment,' *Annals of Economics and Statistics* 113/114, 121–57.

Boadway, Robin and Katherine Cuff (2015), 'Tax Treatment of Bequests when Donor Benefits are Discounted,' *International Tax and Public Finance* 22, 604–34.

Boadway, Robin and Katherine Cuff (2018), 'Optimal Unemployment Insurance and Redistribution,' *Journal of Public Economic Theory* 20, 303–24.

Boadway, Robin and Katherine Cuff (2019), 'Designing a Basic Income: Lessons from the Optimal Income Tax Literature,' paper prepared for the British Columbia Basic Income Expert Committee, British Columbia Ministry of Social Development and Poverty Reduction.

Boadway, Robin, Katherine Cuff and Maurice Marchand (2000a), 'Optimal Income Taxation with Quasi-Linear Preferences Revisited,' *Journal of Public Economic Theory* 2, 435–60.

Boadway, Robin and Laurence Jacquet (2008), 'Optimal Marginal and Average Income Tax Rates under Maximin,' *Journal of Economic Theory* 143, 425–41.

Boadway, Robin, Nicolas Marceau and Motohiro Sato (1999), 'Agency and the Design of Welfare Systems,' *Journal of Public Economics* 73, 1–30.

Boadway, Robin, Maurice Marchand, Pierre Pestieau and Maria del Mar Racionero (2000b), 'Optimal Redistribution with Heterogeneous Preferences for Leisure,' *Journal of Public Economic Theory* 4, 475–98.

Boadway, Robin and Nicolas-Guillaume Martineau (2016), 'Optimal Redistribution with Endogenous Social Norms,' *The Scandinavian Journal of Economics* 118(3), 524–56.

Boadway, Robin and Pierre Pestieau (2007), 'Tagging and Redistributive Taxation,' *Annales d' Economie et de Statistique* 83/84, 2–25.

Boadway, Robin and Anwar Shah (2009), *Fiscal Federalism: Principles and Practice of Multiorder Governance* (Cambridge: Cambridge University Press).

Boone, Jan and A. Lans Bovenberg (2013), 'Optimal Taxation and Welfare Benefits with Monitoring of Job-Search,' *International Tax and Public Finance* 20, 268–92.

Bourguignon, François and Amedeo Spadaro (2012), 'Tax-Benefit Revealed Social Preferences,' *Journal of Economic Inequality* 10, 75–108.

Bovenberg, A. Lans and Bas Jacobs (2005), 'Redistribution and Education Subsidies are Siamese Twins,' *Journal of Public Economics* 89, 2005–35.

Chetty, Raj (2008), 'Moral Hazard versus Liquidity and Optimal Unemployment Insurance,' *Journal of Political Economy* 116, 173–234.

Chetty, Raj (2009), 'Is the Taxable Income Elasticity Sufficient to Calculate Deadweight Loss? The Implications of Evasion and Avoidance,' *American Economic Journal: Economic Policy* 1, 31–52.

Chetty, Raj and Emmanuel Saez (2013), 'Teaching the Tax Code: Earnings Responses to an Experiment with EITC Recipients,' *American Economic Journal: Applied Economics* 5, 1–31.

Choné, Philippe and Guy Laroque (2005), 'Optimal Incentives for Labor Force Participation,' *Journal of Public Economics* 89, 395–425.

Choné, Philippe and Guy Laroque (2010), 'Negative Marginal Tax Rates and Heterogeneity,' *American Economic Review* 100(5), 2532–47.

Choné, Philippe and Guy Laroque (2011), 'Optimal Taxation in the Extensive Model,' *Journal of Economic Theory* 146, 425–53.

Christiansen, Vidar (2015), 'Optimal Participation Taxes,' *Economica* 82, 595–612.

Christiansen, Vidar and Eilev S. Jansen (1978), 'Implicit Social Preferences in the Norwegian System of Indirect Taxation,' *Journal of Public Economics* 10, 217–45.

Christiansen, Vidar and Stephen Smith (2021), *Economic Principles of Commodity Taxation*, Elements in Public Economics (Cambridge: Cambridge University Press).

Corlett, W. J. and D. C. Hague (1953), 'Complementarity and the Excess Burden of Taxation,' *Review of Economic Studies* 21, 21–30.

Cremer, Helmuth, Firouz Gahvari and Jean-Marie Lozachmeur (2010), 'Tagging and Income Taxation: Theory and an Application,' *American Economic Journal: Economic Policy* 2, 31–50.

Cremer, Helmuth and Pierre Pestieau (2011), 'The Tax Treatment of Intergenerational Wealth Transfer,' *CESifo Economic Studies* 57, 365–401.

Cuff, Katherine (2000), 'Optimality of Workfare with Heterogeneous Preferences,' *Canadian Journal of Economics* 33, 149–74.

Dahlby, Bev (2008), *The Marginal Cost of Public Finds: Theory and Applications* (Cambridge, MA: MIT Press).

Deaton, Angus (1979), 'Optimally Uniform Commodity Taxes,' *Economics Letters* 2, 357–61.

Diamond, Peter A. (1980), 'Income Taxation with Fixed Hours of Work,' *Journal of Public Economics* 13, 101–10.

Diamond, Peter A. (1998), 'Optimal Income Taxation: An Example with a U-Shaped Pattern of Optimal Marginal Tax Rates,' *American Economic Review* 88, 83–95.

Diamond, Peter A. (2006), 'Optimal Tax Treatment of Private Contributions for Public Goods with and without Warm Glow Preferences,' *Journal of Public Economics* 90, 897–919.

Diamond, Peter A. and James A. Mirrlees (1971), 'Optimal Taxation and Public Production I: Production Efficiency and II: Tax Rules,' *American Economic Review* 61, 8–27 and 261–78.

Diamond, Peter A. and Emmanuel Saez (2011), 'The Case for a Progressive Tax: From Basic Research to Policy Recommendations,' *Journal of Economic Perspectives* 25, 165–90.

Edwards, Jeremy, Michael Keen and Matti Tuomala (1994), 'Income Tax, Commodity Taxes and Public Good Provision: A Brief Guide,' *FinanzArchiv* 51, 472–97.

Elster, Jon (1989), 'Social Norms and Economic Theory,' *Journal of Economic Perspectives* 3, 99–117.

Farhi, Emmanuel and Xavier Gabaix (2020), 'Optimal Taxation with Behavioral Agents,' *American Economic Review* 110, 298–336.

Feldstein, Martin (2012), 'The Mirrlees Review,' *Journal of Economic Literature* 50, 781–90.

Feldstein, Martin S. (1976), 'On the Theory of Tax Reform,' *Journal of Public Economics* 6, 77–104.

Feldstein, Martin S. (1999), 'Tax Avoidance and the Deadweight Loss of the Income Tax,' *Review of Economics and Statistics* 81, 674–80.

Fleurbaey, Marc and François Maniquet (2011), *A Theory of Fairness and Social Welfare* (New York: Cambridge University Press).

Fong, Christina (2001), 'Social Preferences, Self-Interest and the Demand for Redistribution,' *Journal of Public Economics* 82, 225–46.

Frank, Robert H. (2005), 'Are Concerns about Relative Income Relevant for Public Policy?' *American Economic Review* 95, 137–41.

Gans, Joshua and Michael Smart (1996), 'Majority Voting with Single Crossing Preferences,' *Journal of Public Economics* 59, 219–37.

Gerritsen, Aart (2016), 'Optimal Taxation when People Do Not Maximize Well-Being,' *Journal of Public Economics* 144, 122–39.

Gordon, Roger and Sarada (2019), *The Role of the Corporation Income*, Elements in Public Economics (Cambridge: Cambridge University Press).

Gordon, Roger H. and Julie Berry Cullen (2012), 'Income Redistribution in a Federal System of Governments,' *Journal of Public Economics* 96, 1100–09.

Grodner, Andrew and Thomas J. Kniesner (2006), 'Social Interactions in Labor Supply,' *Journal of the European Economic Association* 4, 1226–48.

Gruber, Jon and Emmanuel Saez (2002), 'The Elasticity of Taxable Income: Evidence and Implications,' *Journal of Public Economics* 84, 1–32.

Guvenen, Fatih, Gueorgui Kambourov, Burhanettin Kuruscu, Sergio Ocampo-Diaz and Daphne Chen (2019), 'Use It or Lose It: Efficiency Gains from Wealth Taxation,' NBER Working Paper No. 26284.

Haig, Robert M. (1921), *The Federal Income Tax* (New York: Columbia University Press).

Hammond, Peter J. (1987), 'Altruism,' in J. Eatwell, M. Milgate and P. Newman (eds.), *The New Palgrave: A Dictionary of Economics*, 1st ed. (Basingstoke: Palgrave Macmillan), 85–87.

Harberger, Arnold C. (1964), 'Taxation, Resource Allocation and Welfare,' in J. Due (ed.), *The Role of Direct and Indirect Taxes in the Federal Revenue System* (Princeton: Princeton University Press), 25–70.

Hellwig, Martin F. (2009), 'A Note on Deaton's Theorem on the Undesirability of Nonuniform Excise Taxation,' *Economic Letters* 105, 186–88.

Hellwig, Martin F. (2010), 'A Generalization of the Atkinson-Stiglitz (1976) Theorem on the Undesirability of Nonuniform Excise Taxation,' *Economic Letters* 108, 156–58.

Hicks, John R. (1946), *Value and Capital*, 2nd ed. (Oxford: Clarendon Press).

Hochman, Harold M. and James D. Rodgers (1969), 'Pareto Optimal Redistribution,' *American Economic Review* 59, 542–57.

Hosios, Arthur J. (1990), 'On the Efficiency of Matching and Related Models of Search and Unemployment,' *Review of Economic Studies* 57, 279–98.

Hungerbühler, Mathias and Etienne Lehmann (2009), 'On the Optimality of a Minimum Wage: New Insights from Optimal Tax Theory,' *Journal of Public Economics* 93, 464–81.

Hungerbühler, Mathias, Etienne Lehmann, Alexis Parmentier and Bruno Van der Linden (2006), 'Optimal Redistributive Taxation in a Search Equilibrium Model,' *Review of Economic Studies* 73, 743–67.

Hvidberg, Kristoffer, Claus Kreiner and Stefanie Stantcheva (2020), 'Social Position and Fairness Views,' NBER Working Paper No. 28099.

Immonen, Rivta, Ravi Kanbur, Michael Keen and Matti Tuomala (1998), 'Tagging and Taxing: The Optimal Use of Categorical and Income Information in Designing Tax/Transfer Schemes,' *Economica* 65, 179–92.

Jacobs, Bas and A. Lans Bovenberg (2010), 'Human Capital and Optimal Positive Taxation of Capital Income,' *International Tax and Public Finance* 17, 451–78.

Jacobs, Bas and A. Lans Bovenberg (2011), 'Optimal Taxation of Human Capital and the Earnings Function,' *Journal of Public Economic Theory* 13, 957–71.

Jacobs, Bas, Egbert L. W. Jongen and Floris T. Zoutman (2017), 'Revealed Social Preferences of Dutch Political Parties,' *Journal of Public Economics* 156, 81–100.

Jacobson, Louis S., Robert J. LaLonde and Daniel G. Sullivan (1993), 'Earnings Losses of Displaced Workers,' *American Economic Review* 83, 685–709.

Jacobson, Louis S., Robert J. LaLonde and Daniel G. Sullivan (2005), 'Is Retraining Displaced Workers a Good Investment?' *Economic Perspectives* 29, 47–66.

Jacquet, Laurence, Etienne Lehmann and Bruno Van der Linden (2013), 'The Optimal Marginal Tax Rates with Both Extensive and Intensive Responses,' *Journal of Economic Theory* 148, 1770–805.

Jacquet, Laurence, Etienne Lehmann and Bruno Van der Linden (2014), 'Optimal Income Taxation with Kalai Wage Bargaining and Endogenous Participation,' *Social Choice and Welfare* 42, 381–402.

Jacquet, Laurence and Bruno Van der Linden (2006), 'The Normative Analysis of Tagging Revisited: Dealing with Stigmatization,' *FinanzArchiv* 62, 168–98.

Kaldor, Nicholas (1955), *An Expenditure Tax* (London: Allen and Unwin).

Kanbur, Ravi and Matti Tuomala (2013), 'Relativity, Inequality, and Optimal Nonlinear Income Taxation,' *International Economic Review* 54, 1199–217.

Kaplow, Louis (2001), 'Horizontal Equity: New Measures, Unclear Principles,' in K. Hassett and G. Hubbard (eds.), *Inequality and Tax Policy* (Washington: American Enterprise Institute), 75–97.

Kaplow, Louis (2006), 'On the Desirability of Commodity Taxation Even when Income Taxation is Not Optimal,' *Journal of Public Economics* 90, 1235–50.

Kaplow, Louis (2008), *The Theory of Taxation and Public Economics* (Princeton: Princeton University Press).

Karni, Edi (1999), 'Optimal Unemployment Insurance: A Survey,' *Southern Economic Journal* 66, 442–65.

Kasy, Maximilian (2018), 'Why a Universal Basic Income is Better than Subsidies of Low-Wage Work,' Data for Progress Working Paper No. 2. http://filesforprogress.org/pdfs/UBI_EITC_Kasy_DFP_Working_Paper.pdf

Keane, Michael P. (2011), 'Labor Supply and Taxes: A Survey,' *Journal of Economic Literature* 49, 961–1075.

Kleven, Henrik Jacobsen (2014), 'How Can Scandinavians Tax So Much?' *Journal of Economic Perspectives* 28, 77–98.

Kleven, Henrik Jacobsen (2019), 'The EITC and the Extensive Margin: A Reappraisal,' Working Paper No. 26405, National Bureau of Economic Research, Cambridge, MA.

Kleven, Henrik Jacobsen and Wojciech Kopczuk (2011), 'Transfer Program Complexity and the Take Up of Social Benefits,' *American Economic Journal: Economic Policy* 3, 54–90.

Kleven, Henrik Jacobsen and Esben Anton Schultz (2014), 'Estimating Taxable Income Responses Using Danish Tax Reforms,' *American Economic Journal: Economic Policy* 6, 271–301.

Kroft, Kory, Kavan Kucko, Etienne Lehmann and Johannes Schmieder (2020), 'Optimal Income Taxation with Unemployment and Wage Responses: A Sufficient Statistics Approach,' *American Economic Journal: Economic Policy* 12, 254–92.

Kuziemko, Ilyana, Michael I. Norton, Emmanuel Saez and Stefanie Stantcheva (2015), 'How Elastic are Preferences for Redistribution? Evidence from Randomized Survey Experiments,' *American Economic Review* 105, 1478–508.

LaLonde, Robert J. (2007), *The Case for Wage Insurance*, Council on Foreign Relations Special Report No. 30 (New York: Council on Foreign Relations).

Landais, Camille, Pascal Michaillat and Emmanuel Saez (2018), 'A Macroeconomic Approach to Optimal Unemployment Insurance: Theory,' *American Economic Journal: Economic Policy* 10, 152–81.

Laroque, Guy (2005), 'Indirect Taxation is Superfluous under Separability and Taste Homogeneity: A Simple Proof,' *Economics Letters* 87, 141–44.

Lavecchia, Adam (2020), 'Minimum Wage Policy with Optimal Taxes and Unemployment,' *Journal of Public Economics* 190, 104–228.

Layard, Richard (1980), 'Human Satisfactions and Public Policy,' *Economic Journal* 90, 737–50.

Lee, David and Emmanuel Saez (2012), 'Optimal Minimum Wage Policy in Competitive Labor Markets,' *Journal of Public Economics* 96, 739–49.

Lehmann, Etienne, Alexis Parmentier and Bruno Van der Linden (2011), 'Optimal Income Taxation with Endogenous Participation and Search Unemployment,' *Journal of Public Economics* 95, 1523–37.

Lockwood, Benjamin B. (2020), 'Optimal Income Taxation with Present Bias,' *American Economic Journal: Economic* Policy 12, 298-327.

Lockwood, Benjamin B. and Matthew Weinzierl (2016), 'Positive and Normative Judgments Implicit in U.S. Tax Policy, and the Costs of Unequal Growth and Recessions,' *Journal of Monetary Economics* 77, 30–47.

Luttmer, Erzo F. P. and Monica Singhal (2014), 'Tax Morale,' *Journal of Economic Perspectives* 28, 149–68.

Marceau, Nicolas and Robin Boadway (1994), 'Minimum Wage Legislation and Unemployment Insurance as Instruments for Redistribution,' *Scandinavian Journal of Economics* 96, 67–81.

Martinez-Vazquez, Jorge and Stanley L. Winer (eds.) (2014), *Coercion and Social Welfare in Public Finance* (New York: Cambridge University Press).

Meade Report (1978), *The Structure and Reform of Direct Taxation*, Report of a Committee Chaired by Professor J. E. Meade (London: Allen and Unwin).

Meltzer, Allan H. and Scott F. Richard (1981), 'A Rational Theory of the Size of Government,' *Journal of Political Economy* 89, 914–27.

Milgrom, Paul (1993), 'Is Sympathy an Economic Value? Philosophy, Economics, and the Contingent Valuation Method,' in J. A. Hausman (ed.), *Contingent Valuation: A Critical Assessment* (Amsterdam: Elsevier), 418–35.

Mirrlees, James, Stuart Adam, Timothy Besley et al. (2011), *Tax by Design: The Mirrlees Review* (Oxford: Oxford University Press).

Mirrlees, James A. (1971), 'An Exploration in the Theory of Optimum Income Taxation,' *Review of Economic Studies* 38, 175–208.

Mirrlees, James A. (2007), 'Taxation of Gifts and Bequests,' slides for a talk at the Centenary of James Meade Conference, mimeo.

Musgrave, Richard A. (1959), *The Theory of Public Finance* (New York: McGraw-Hill).

Nava, Mario, Fred Schroyen and Maurice Marchand (1996), 'Optimal Fiscal and Public Expenditure Policy in a Two-Class Economy,' *Journal of Public Economics* 61, 119–37.

Newbery, David M. (1986), 'On the Desirability of Input Taxes,' *Economics Letters* 20, 267–70.

Nishimura, Yukihiro (2003), 'Optimal Commodity Taxation for the Reduction of Envy,' *Social Choice and Welfare* 21, 501–27.

Olivera, Javier (2015), 'Preferences for Redistribution in Europe,' *IZA Journal of European Labor Studies* 4, 1–18.

Osborne, Martin J. and Al Slivinski (1996), 'A Model of Political Competition with Citizen-Candidates,' *Quarterly Journal of Economics* 111, 65–96.

Oswald, Andrew (1983), 'Altruism, Jealousy and the Theory of Optimal Non-Linear Taxation,' *Journal of Public Economics* 20, 77–87.

Parsons, Donald O. (1996), 'Imperfect "Tagging" in Social Insurance Programs,' *Journal of Public Economics* 62, 183–207.

Piketty, Thomas and Emmanuel Saez (2013), 'Optimal Labor Income Taxation,' in A. Auerbach, R. Chetty, M. Feldstein and E. Saez (eds.), *Handbook of Public Economics*, Volume 5 (Amsterdam: North Holland), 391–474.

Pissarides, Christopher A. (2000), *Equilibrium Unemployment Theory*, 2nd ed. (Cambridge, MA: MIT Press).

President's Advisory Panel on Federal Tax Reform (2005), *Simple, Fair and Pro-Growth: Proposals to Fix America's Tax System* (Washington, DC: U.S. Treasury).

Ramsey, Frank P. (1927), 'A Contribution to the Theory of Taxation,' *Economic Journal* 37, 47–61.

Roemer, John E. (1998), *Equality of Opportunity* (Cambridge, MA: Harvard University Press).

Rogerson, Richard, Robert Shimer and Randall Wright (2005), 'Search-Theoretic Models of the Labor Market: A Survey,' *Journal of Economic Literature* 43, 959–88.

Rothschild, Casey and Florin Scheuer (2013), 'Redistributive Taxation in the Roy Model,' *Quarterly Journal of Economics* 128, 623–68.

Rothstein, Jesse (2010), 'Is the EITC as Good as an NIT? Conditional Cash Transfers and Tax Incidence,' *American Economic Policy: Economic Policy* 2, 177–208.

Royal Commission on Taxation (1966), *Report* (The Carter Report) (Ottawa: Queen's Printer).

Royal Commission on the Taxation of Profits and Income (1955), *Report* (London: Her Majesty's Stationery Office).

Saez, Emmanuel (2001), 'Using Elasticities to Derive Optimal Income Tax Rates,' *Review of Economic Studies* 68, 205–09.

Saez, Emmanuel (2002), 'Optimal Income Transfer Programs: Intensive vs Extensive Labor Supply Responses,' *Quarterly Journal of Economics* 117, 1039–73.

Saez, Emmanuel (2010), 'Do Taxpayers Bunch at Kink Points?' *American Economic Journal: Economic Policy* 2, 180–212.

Saez, Emmanuel, Joel Slemrod and Seth Giertz (2012), 'The Elasticity of Taxable Income with Respect to Marginal Tax Rates: A Critical Review,' *Journal of Economic Literature* 50, 3–50.

Saez, Emmanuel and Stefanie Stantcheva (2016), 'Generalized Social Marginal Welfare Weights for Optimal Tax Theory,' *American Economic Review* 106, 24–45.

Saez, Emmanuel and Michael Veall (2005), 'The Evolution of High Incomes in Northern America: Lessons from Canadian Evidence,' *American Economic Review* 95, 831–49.

Samuelson, Paul A. (1986), 'Theory of Optimal Taxation,' *Journal of Public Economics* 30, 137–43.

Sandmo, Agnar (1976), 'Optimal Taxation: An Introduction to the Literature,' *Journal of Public Economics* 6, 37–54.

Schanz, George von (1896), 'Der Einkommensbegriff und die Einkommensteuergesetze,' *FinanzArchiv* 13, 1–87.

Scheuer, Florian and Joel Slemrod (2021), 'Taxing our Wealth,' *Journal of Economic Perspectives* 35, 207–30.

Sen, Amartya (1973), *On Economic Inequality* (Oxford: Clarendon Press).

Sheshinski, Eytan (1972), 'The Optimal Linear Income Tax,' *Review of Economic Studies* 39, 297–302.

Simons, Henry C. (1938), *Personal Income Taxation* (Chicago: University of Chicago Press).

Slemrod, Joel, Shlomo Yitzhaki, Joram Mayshar and Michael Lundholm (1994), 'The Optimal Two-Bracket Linear Income Tax,' *Journal of Public Economics* 53, 269–90.

Spadaro, Amedeo, Luca Piccoli and Lucia Mangiavacchi (2015), 'Optimal Taxation, Social Preferences and the Four Worlds of Welfare Capitalism in Europe,' *Economica* 82, 448–85.

Spinnewijn, Johannes (2015), 'Unemployed but Optimistic: Optimal Insurance Design with Biased Beliefs,' *Journal of the European Economic Association* 13, 130–67.

Stantcheva, Stefanie (2015), 'Learning and (or) Doing: Human Capital Investments and Optimal Taxation,' NBER Working Paper No. 21381.

Stiglitz, Joseph E. (1982), 'Self-Selection and Pareto Efficient Taxation,' *Journal of Public Economics* 17, 213–40.

Tanninen, Hannu, Matti Tuomala and Elina Tuominen (2019), *Inequality and Optimal Redistribution*, Elements in Public Economics (Cambridge: Cambridge University Press).

Tarroux, Benoît (2019), 'The Value of Tax Progressivity: Evidence from Survey Experiments,' *Journal of Public Economics* 179, Article No. 104068.

Tuomala, Matti (2016), *Optimal Redistributive Taxation* (Oxford: Oxford University Press).

United States Treasury (1977), *Blueprints for Basic Tax Reform* (Washington, DC: Government Printing Office).

Veall, Michael (2012), 'Top Income Shares in Canada: Recent Trends and Policy Implications,' *Canadian Journal of Economics* 45, 1247–72.

Weinzierl, Matthew (2014), 'The Promise of Positive Optimal Taxation: Normative Diversity and a Role for Equal Sacrifice,' *Journal of Public Economics* 118, 128–42.

Weinzierl, Matthew C. (2011), 'The Surprising Power of Age-Dependent Taxes,' *Review of Economic Studies* 78, 1490–518.

Wenzel, Michael (2005), 'Motivation or Rationalisation? Causal Relations between Ethics, Norms and Tax Compliance,' *Journal of Economic Psychology* 26, 491–508.

Wicksell, Knut (1896), *Finanztheoretische Untersuchungen* (Jena: Gustav Fischer); translated as 'A New Principle of Just Taxation,' in R. Musgrave and A. T. Peacock (eds.), *Classics in the Theory of Public Finance* (New York: St. Martin's Press), 72–118.

Woittiez, Isolde and Arie Kapteyn (1998), 'Social Interactions and Habit Formation in a Model of Female Labour Supply,' *Journal of Public Economics* 70, 185–205.

Acknowledgements

This Element draws on Boadway and Cuff (2019). David Green, Yiannis Kipouros, Barnabas Ney, and two referees provided helpful comments and assistance. Financial support from the British Columbia Ministry of Social Development and Poverty Reduction is gratefully acknowledged.

Cambridge Elements ☰

Public Economics

Robin Boadway
Queen's University

Robin Boadway is Emeritus Professor of Economics at Queen's University. His main research interests are in public economics, welfare economics, and fiscal federalism.

Frank A. Cowell
The London School of Economics and Political Science

Frank A. Cowell is Professor of Economics at the London School of Economics. His main research interests are in inequality, mobility, and the distribution of income and wealth.

Massimo Florio
University of Milan

Massimo Florio is Professor of Public Economics at the University of Milan. His main interests are in cost-benefit analysis, regional policy, privatization, public enterprise, network industries, and the socio-economic impact of research infrastructures.

About the Series

The Cambridge Elements of Public Economics provides authoritative and up-to-date reviews of core topics and recent developments in the field. It includes state-of-the-art contributions on all areas in the field. The editors are particularly interested in the new frontiers of quantitative methods in public economics, experimental approaches, behavioral public finance, empirical, and theoretical analysis of the quality of government and institutions.

Cambridge Elements$^{\equiv}$

Public Economics

Elements in the Series

CPSIA information can be obtained
at www.ICGtesting.com
Printed in the USA
BVHW052152190123
656703BV00021B/352